W0115313

BLUE MESA REVIEW

ISSUE 22
SPRING 2009

The Creative Writing Program
University of New Mexico

BLUE MESA REVIEW
The Creative Writing Program
University of New Mexico
MSC03-2170, Humanities 274
Albuquerque, NM 87131-0001

Fax: 505.277.0021
Email: bmrinfo@unm.edu

$[c \, l \, m \, p]$ member

BLUE MESA REVIEW is the literary magazine of the Creative Writing
Program at the University of New Mexico. Funding is provided by the
College of Arts & Sciences and the Department of English Language
and Literature.

MANUSCRIPTS are accepted year-round, but the editorial board does
not read work during the summer months. For complete guidelines,
visit our website at www.unm.edu/~bluemesa.

COVER IMAGE: Suzanne Sbarge *Still Life*
Mixed media on panel, 16 x 16 inches
Courtesy of Nüart Gallery, Santa Fe, New Mexico
www.nuartgallery.com

BLUE MESA REVIEW is indexed through the American Humanities
Index.

Blue Mesa Review is
sponsored by the
New Mexico
Humanities Council.

New Mexico Humanities Council

BLUE MESA REVIEW

SPRING 2009
ISSUE 22

EDITOR IN CHIEF
Chris Wrenn

MANAGING EDITOR
Samantha Tetangco

PRODUCTION EDITOR
Alyssa Christy

FICTION EDITOR
Melanie Unruh

POETRY EDITOR
Kyle Churney

NONFICTION EDITOR
Linda Rickert

COPY EDITOR
Marisa P. Clark

INTERNS
Fiction: Lenore Gusch and Monet Maloof
Poetry: Adrianne Hopper
Nonfiction: Brett Elwell
Production: Leslie Fishburn-Clark and
Kimberly Keller

READERS
Joe D. Byrne, Ryan Cheshire, Dan Darling,
Aaron Espinosa, Emily Haynes, Jennifer
Krohn, Casandra Lopez, Claudia O'Keefe,
Bob Sabatini, K. Andrew Turner, and
Tanaya Winder

TABLE OF CONTENTS

FICTION

POETRY

NONFICTION

SHOSTAKOVICH AT THE FLYING STAR CAFÉ

BY MAUREEN SEATON

(After String Quartet No. 1 in C Major, Op 49)

Everything has its limit, including sorrow.—Joseph Brodsky

My mother was smitten with your pathos and your rapid pulse.
　　She whispered your name like an Olympian's,

　　　　loved you through Stalin, McCarthy,
　　Kennedy and Khrushchev, between her own daily operas

of *Guiding Light* and *Search for Tomorrow*, Joy
　　for dishes, Spic and Span for kitchen floors.

　　　　When they denounced you a second time, I'd been born
　　in Jersey, the first of my mother's hopefuls—

pizzicato in the second movement,
　　irony in the third, recapitulation in the fourth.

　　　　We were her sheltered American brood, her four
　　melancholy variations. You were her maestro.

She fed us meatloaf and wistful preludes, and we
　　memorized her terror and her grief.

　　　　At fourteen I rebelled and consented to Stravinsky,
　　Prokoviev, Gershwin—any Russian but hers.

Then I left the motherland altogether—
　　for Satie and Debussy, Joni and Dylan.

　　　　You said, of your first quartet, that you *visualized*
　　childhood scenes...bright moods associated with spring.

Now it's raining on the Flying Star patio, the rain I've
   come to delight in since defecting to the desert.

     I'm in earphones under a wide umbrella,
   absorbed in the climax of viola and cello,

violins driving the major chord home.
   I can't hear you and not think of her,

     a woman who lived and died in the key
   of C-sharp minor, remote and almost glowing,

a ruby deep in the matrix of her time.
   Listen to your transgressive strings, the way they

     hold my heart and pound it. There was a day, long ago,
   when you and I entered a soundproof booth

and blocked out the entire world.
   Now there's a hush everywhere but inside me.

     The rain sounds sacred as it hits the implacable earth.

THE END OF THE MAYAN CALENDAR

BY STEVEN RAMIREZ

2009 FICTION CONTEST AWARD WINNER

On foot, you can still leave this country for twenty-five cents. It just takes longer.

The first time I did it I was thirteen and I'd lied to my mother, told her I was going to a *quinceañera* downtown, and me and Carlos and Isaac and Paul parked a stolen car in Mama's lot, counted our change and crossed the bridge only to end up at the Mariachi bar because from there we could still see the blue and yellow lights of our neighborhoods. We asked for one beer each and when the bartender didn't flinch we tripled our order. One minute and twelve seconds later we were arm in arm, singing along with the music from the jukebox because we'd heard the song a million times before. This was our bar now, we agreed, and right then a group of men in Dallas Cowboys jerseys stormed in, pulled an old man off his stool and kicked him in the face and ribs until he wasn't moving anymore. They left just as quickly and when the bartender came to our table Isaac looked at him and in a low voice said, "Drugs?"

The bartender laughed and asked for our IDs and when we couldn't produce them he laughed harder and brought us twelve more beers.

You hear stories about Mexico—those'll cost you nothing—stories about the Crooked Cops in Aviators, kidnappings, slave labor, gun fights, ritual killings, whores as old as your grandma blowing men in alleyways, houses made of car tires, houses made of gold, the major drug families—Fuentes, Zaragoza, Romero—bodies of women and children buried beneath acres of undeveloped land, but the stories, countless as they are, seem like far away disasters—civilization-ending, yes, but not ours, no, not ours—like section D-8 reports in the newspaper about meteors colliding or stars exploding or entire galaxies being sucked into black holes, silent as bathwater and ten billion light years away.

And you begin to think that the old man in the Mariachi bar didn't get it so bad, a few healthy kicks here and there, nothing you wouldn't experience playing YMCA soccer, probably a small misunderstanding, you think, or maybe he had it coming and he's sitting in another bar at this very moment, laughing about the entire thing, thanking God it was the Dallas Cowboys and not the Chicago Bears because now *those* guys can play. And suddenly, you find a quarter under your pillow and you're ready to go back.

I had a best friend we called The Brain because he was smart as shit—math awards, chess club, honor roll, card carrying member of The Young Einstein Society, MENSA, pre-med track since the second grade, five-time winner of the Doogie Howser Award, and he'd even memorized the dictionary, no joke, the entire thing, and I liked to test him by cracking open the especially fat ones and shooting large Martian words in his direction. *Coelenterate, flageolet, gymkhana, Hanukkah.* He knew them each time, definition and spelling, this root and that, and he'd laugh at me and explain that these words were more common than I thought, that I could hear them all around me in Dolby Digital if I just opened my ears for one goddamn second and listened!

On his fifteenth birthday I introduced him to Mama and we crossed the bridge, passed the Mariachi bar and ended up at an eight-dollar drink-and-drown happening at Alive, Alive, Alive! We drank vodka from Styrofoam cups until our faces became a matching shade of blue, then purple. This was fun, we agreed, more fun than Webster's goddamn dictionary and Brain laughed at that one until he vomited all over the dance floor but no one seemed to notice. There were Carlos and Isaac and Paul at the bar, finger-banging a woman twice our age and it was Mrs. Valdez, our French teacher, and everyone in the place, we realized, was from our side of the bridge, dancing, dancing, dancing, and Carlos said to me, "Yeah, dude, I just saw your mom going into the women's restroom," and I told him I'd just seen his going into the men's. He shrugged. "Hey, Brain," he said. "Why don't you spell for us *ee-nee-bree-ay-shun*?" We laughed and raised our Styrofoam cups and sang Happy Birthday. We left Mrs. Valdez and sank deeper into the strip because it was time to get The Brain laid. We stopped at a pink house, the front door lit only by an active bug-zapper, and the sleepy-eyed women lined up before us were just not going to do. "Younger," we shouted at the small man wearing gold bracelets. "Younger, younger, younger! Y-O-U-N-G-E-R!" And because we'd asked for it, he returned with a girl who might as well have been his daughter and we pushed The Brain into her and into her.

Afterwards, back in Mama's lot, The Brain and I sat in his car waiting for our vision to steady. He stared out his window, up toward the sky.

"Something's coming," he said. "I'd say we asked for it but it's been coming all along, like days and weeks and months."

"An alien invasion?" I laughed. "Should I call the President?"

"There's nothing alien about it," he said dryly. "That's the thing. It's complete and natural progress."

"Is there a word for that?" I said, trying to lighten the mood.

The Brain shrugged. "Fuck if I know," he said and started the car.

Six hundred years ago men dressed in tin arrived on the shores of the Yucatán Peninsula, the size of their ships matched only by the gleam of their blue and hungry eyes, and they'd come a long distance, fueled by an additional hundred years' worth of stories, mysterious stories, invisible in origin as if engendered by the wind itself, stories of precious metals, of cities the color of the rising sun, of so much land throbbing with life, not to mention the hundreds of thousands of wandering souls in need of salvation and what better way to commence this salvation than to strap a crucifix to their necks, plug a tool into their hands and set them to worship and work, in that order.

Imagine their surprise, then, when not two minutes into their conquest the Men in Tin realized that there were no precious metals, that the cities were there, yes, but they were made of dull and silent stone, that nothing inhabited this land but a faint echo and that they'd crossed an ocean just to discover once again that we are all alone.

There was one thing, however.

At the center of a black forest they uncovered a calendar that counted time according to the movements of the stars and planets. And while the calendar would go on and on, beyond the lives of their children and their children's children and the children after that, it was marked in the middle—a clear division of before and after—by a crude etching of a man wrapped in his own long beard. And suddenly the Men in Tin felt their own understanding of the world shrink, and shrink, until it was the size of the shells beneath their feet. And then they began to shrink, and shrink, until they could barely stand beneath the weight of their armor, and they knew then that the only way to reverse this process was to send word home that yes—*yes!*—they'd found exactly what they were looking for.

On foot, you can still leave this country for twenty-five cents.

Returning will cost you about as much, plus one magic word and it sure as hell isn't *please*.

I was with Jaime Rincon and we'd just spent all our birthday and Christmas and Grandma money at the OTB and when we reached the border an agent with square shoulders, face, and haircut glared at us, waiting for us to spit it out, and Jaime—feeling no doubt electric from the liquid heroin we'd pounded minutes before at The Derby because the night wasn't going to be a complete loss— spread the corners of his eyes with his fingers and shouted, "*Japones!*"

The agent drove the butt of his gun into Jaime's face and pushed him back, back, back until I could no longer see him.

Darrius Scott spent an entire afternoon at a massage parlor in celebration of a scholarship to a PAC-10 school—or was it Big 12?—and on his way back the agent looked him up and down and said, "Where you been, boy?" and Darrius spit on the agent's shoes and said, "On top of your mama. Boy."

Carlos had been returning with three gallons of *Horchata*, which was immediately confiscated, and when asked for the magic word he snarled at the agent and said, "My dad signs your checks."

My brother Gibran had been returning with something other than *Horchata*, something that fit snug between his underwear and nut sack and crack of his ass, and before the agent could say a thing, my brother shouted, "Fuck you, fuck you, fuck you!" and I don't know why he did that, guilt I suppose, but if anything, he did avoid drug charges.

There are hundreds and thousands of us who don't belong on the other side of that bridge—we belong in bed, in college, at a breakfast table, in jail, but not there, no, anywhere but there—but when the time comes to stand up straight, look the square agent square in his square eyes and repeat the magic word, something happens, and we forget the word. It eludes us. Or we simply don't want to say it altogether because six-hundred and some odd years later we still haven't found what we're looking for.

So we say, *thanks but no thanks, officer, fuck you* and *I think I'll stay a bit longer.*

You don't have to be a member of the Young Einstein Society to know that time and space are funny things. In the night sky we see light from stars that have been dead for billions of years. And we wish upon this light. We draw pictures with our fingers, connecting this dot and that, until the light becomes a fish, a bull, an archer, a reflection of us.

The sunlight in our sky is eight minutes younger than the sun itself—a mere echo of something that has come and gone and will never return again. Upon this echo we map out our days and weeks and months and years. On our bedside calendars we cross off time that was never there to begin with. The sun might have already aligned with the center of the galaxy, expanded and consumed this planet in one red wave and we wouldn't know it for another eight silent minutes.

The news crossed the border on a Sunday morning and landed on my kitchen table in wet print. *La Limpia,* the papers called it, and they warned us to stay put, whatever you do, do not cross the bridge—in fact, steer clear altogether because the violence has spread, it said. There is no border and we are no longer safe.

The Crooked Cops in Aviators had declared war on the drug families and the drug families had retaliated and the crossfire had overflowed and anyone who got in the way—a trip to the grocery store, a morning jog, a Sunday drive with the top down—was sure to suffer accordingly. By the time I finished the last Cheerio the stories had risen from the print like fumes and I breathed them in until they were a part of me and I'd known them my entire life.

A boy two years older than me, who'd gone to my high school and broken his share of track records, had crossed to visit his grandfather only to be gunned down at the intersection of Zapata and Avenida de las Americas.

Martha, a woman with bleached blonde hair who had collected the eight-dollar cover outside of USA Connection since I could remember, had been led to an alleyway by two men in cowboy hats, and executed.

The Mariachi bar had burned to the ground.

The chief of police's head had been spotted floating in a fountain like a child's bath toy.

And Mama: slumped against her halogen-lit booth, a wad of bills in both hands, a distant look in her gray eyes, and some people claimed strangulation, or poison, but then again she was old as dirt and maybe it was just her time.

I washed my bowl in the sink. I drank an entire Coke in one gulp and recycled the can. The silence was killing me.

I searched the couch cushions for quarters and hopped into my mother's car.

There's no answer as to what became of the Mayan Civilization. Just that by the time the Spanish arrived, they were gone—out, split, see ya and *vamanos!* This part's inarguable. Fact. What's debated, however, is the oldest question in recorded history and that is: What the hell happened? Plague? Famine? Migration? Revolt? Astro-collision? Aliens from the planet Neptune scooping them aboard their shiny discs and taking them for an intergalactic field trip?

What happened, what happened, what happened?

The Men in Tin didn't know then and we certainly don't know now. All we know is that when the ships came ashore, when the would-be conquerors entered that black forest with their blades out before them, they found, among the deserted cities and shrines and pagan relics, the movement of our universe. And at the center of this universe—having nothing to do with what was manifest or anointed by God Himself—they saw themselves. The dull and linear truth.

On foot, you can still leave this country for twenty-five cents.

When you arrive on the other side, you will not fear. You will take everything you've ever learned and you will recognize—in the faces of the Crooked Cops in Aviators, the cigarette vendors, the drug families, the whores as old as your grandma, the bodies scattered up and down the avenues like bags of sand, the children hawking *chicharones* and Chiclets along the bridge—the faces of everyone you've ever known. Carlos and Isaac and Paul and Mama and The Brain and Mrs. Valdez and Jaime Rincon and Darrius Scott and the square-faced agents and Martha and your brother.

You'll see yourself. And you'll snap your fingers and think, *Okay!* and *Yes!* and *I Get it Now! We did this, we did this, we did this!* and just before you pat yourself on the back and call yourself Charlton Heston from *Planet of the Apes* a little boy in torn white pants will approach you, and suddenly you'll want to buy his Chiclets—hell, you'll even let him keep the change—and as you present the crisp five-dollar bill, he raises his tiny fist and punches you right in the balls and shouts, "*¡Vuelva a tu lado, cabron!*"

And you will. Because the violence isn't what you expected. And you brought extra quarters.

You always do.

Congratulations to the finalists for the 2009 Fiction Prize: Ryan Habermeyer, Rachel Eve Moulton, and Beth Piatote.

This year's contest was judged by Barry Kitterman. He has taught writing and literature at IU East, Miami University of Ohio, and at two universities in the People's Republic of China, Nankai and Qingdao. In 1989-90 he was Hudson Walker fellow at the Fine Arts Work Center in Provincetown, MA. Since 1994, he has taught at Austin Peay State University in Clarksville, TN, where he currently coordinates the creative writing program and the visiting writers series. He has published short fiction and nonfiction in The Carolina Quarterly, The Chariton Review, Turnstile, Flyway and elsewhere. He is the fiction editor for *Zone 3 Magazine* (APSU) and is an associate editor of The Green Hills Literary Lantern (Truman State University). In 2001, he received an individual artist's grant from the Tennessee Arts Commission. His novel *The Baker's Boy* was published in May 2008. He lives with his wife, Jill Eichhorn, and their two children, Teddy and Hannah, in Clarksville, Tennessee.

THE THEORY OF DOG SHIT

BY GARY FINCKE

Old man Krause was one of those neighbors we thought we hated. Because he came outside to curse at us when a foul ball rolled into his yard. Because he'd hidden behind his shrubbery once and leapt out to pounce on a rolling softball, refusing to return it.

One afternoon, while we sat around complaining about adults, Charlie Schneider explained the theory of dog shit, how a burning bag full would draw the people we targeted to their front porches where the men, especially, would stamp out the fire while we watched happily from a safely distant shadow. It seemed like such a great idea that the next weekend, Dave Tolley and I watched Charlie scoop a week's worth of his golden retriever's dog turds into a paper sack and followed him across the vacant lot where we played to stand beside him in the summer darkness while he lit the bag and rang old man Krause's bell.

We hid on the street side of the same shrubbery Krause had used earlier in the week. But when Krause flung open the door, he didn't stomp on the fire. He just yelled at us. "I know who you are. Young Tolley and Schneider. I know your fathers."

I was glad to be excluded because I didn't live on the same street, but we didn't bother Krause any more that summer. Instead, we tried the theory of dog shit on a dozen enemy houses—the fathers of effeminate classmates and girls who ignored us, but mostly men who trimmed their lawns so perfectly and so often we thought we hated them as much as we did a softball stealer. We moved out of their neighborhood and mine to give our victims more would-be vandals from whom to choose, and though there were men who cursed into the darkness, launching the great obscenities of anger, not once did the person who answered the door step on the bag of shit.

It was the summer of 1959, we'd just finished eighth grade, and a whole new set of neighbors had moved in during the past two years because the farm between my house and the housing plan where Dave Tolley, Charlie Schneider, and old man Krause lived had been sold and divided into lots. Three years earlier, when there were huge drainage pipes set in place to accommodate the changes in landscape and the demands of sixty new families, we'd used those pipes to entertain ourselves.

Each one of the pipes eventually led downhill to The Flats, where the township's poorest families lived. Pine Creek, which flowed among those houses, flooded them each spring. There was an abandoned strip mine at one end of that neighborhood and a busy highway bordered another side. All three of us could see that drainage from the housing plan would empty itself onto the hillside above The Flats, one more reason to be happy to live on high ground, although never once did we burn dog shit on the front porches of those who lived there.

What we did was crabwalk through those enormous storm drains, pretending we were following a lead-lined tunnel to a bomb shelter like the ones people were beginning to build because the Russians were threatening to nuke us. Overhead the model home that had been built before any of the lots were sold was unlocked for the wives of steelworkers and mechanics and truck drivers, men who worked with their hands like our fathers did. Once, we'd watched those women brush their fingertips over the slick Braille of appliances before they parted the gold and green patterned drapes to appreciate the view, but quickly, in the dark, we forgot the simple geography of the corridor, and all three of us raised our voices as if volume was a vaccine for the sudden amnesia of being underground.

We couldn't get ourselves properly turned around. For ten minutes we sweated and swore our mild, fifth-grade oaths like "damn" and "hell" and "shit," and finally we skidded out of a pipe fifty feet above a back yard full of old tires and two abandoned cars.

One neighbor we didn't harass was Jack Hall, who was building a bomb shelter in his back yard because he was a veteran of nuclear testing and said he knew exactly what was coming for the families whose fathers thought the only possible use for the A-bomb after Hiroshima and Nagasaki was stock footage in movies and television shows.

He'd done a hitch at Camp Desert Rock, where he'd witnessed a bomb test called Shot Smoky by standing in the open with a group of other soldiers four miles from the tower where the A-bomb ignited. He'd watched two other earlier tests and been discharged shortly after Shot Smoky with sores and loose teeth, dizzy enough, he told us five times that summer, to tumble down his own steps like a baby.

"Like a hurricane full of shit," he told us. "Dirt and wire, sagebrush, rattlesnakes, and what not. We hugged God's good earth and then we stood up and marched to ground zero to make sure that tower and everything around it looked like nothing."

He talked to us because we stopped to see how his shelter was coming along. Our fathers didn't work evenings and weekends on a place to hide when the missiles were launched. They didn't say a word about the duck-and-cover we learned in school, nothing about doing what our junior high school teachers taught, nothing whatsoever about purified water and canned food, generators, a thick cement wall, and the rest of what Jack Hall's family would have by the end of the summer. Better to "go like that," they said, using the finger snap my mother made to demonstrate the way an old woman on our street had died just after school had ended.

That summer the Congress reaffirmed something called the Captive Nations Resolution. The newspaper said it had been passed in 1953, and Eisenhower, for the seventh time, was proclaiming a week of prayer for those under Communism. "Good timing," my father said, "what with Nixon off to the Soviet Union. Maybe he'll lead them all in prayer."

I didn't care about Nixon's trip, but I worried that my father would announce there were evening church services to insure the community's compliance with prayer. That the government's edict would end up with me enduring another week like the one before Easter, a second Holy Thursday service, the Good Friday three-hour marathon, and worse, sunrise service, getting up at 5:30 to sing the praises of democracy, filing out to the breakfast of pancakes and sausages before we filed back in for Sunday school and regular church.

In Moscow, Nixon and Kruschev argued among the dishwashers and televisions in the pavilion on technology sponsored by the USA. The United States, Kruschev blustered, was a bourgeois department store. "Good," my mother said, watching the news. Nixon didn't have to tell us the USSR was an armory. In Florida, that week, to show how likely it was for the Soviets to launch an attack, newlyweds named Minison were spending their honeymoon in a bomb shelter exclusively for *Life* magazine. We could expect the photographs soon.

Later that week Jack Hall's nearly completed bomb shelter, after the summer's heaviest rain, flooded like the root cellar under our porch. "If there's a war," my father said, "they'll be in the soup, all right, only it will be radioactive broth."

For once I thought my father was right. He knew as much about survival as anyone on the streets I could walk to, including Jack Hall. He was a Scoutmaster, and everything he owned for Boy Scouts was survival gear—flashlights, canteens, first aid kits, lanterns.

None of it seemed like it would help anybody last for the next seventy years like I wanted to, but the nearby hardware store sold a crowbar as an "instant fallout shelter" because, their sign said, you could use it to pry open a manhole cover and clamber down to safety. "Fat chance," my father said. We hadn't ever gone back into the confusing storm drains, but now, because we knew it would lead to manholes, my friends and I entered the mouth of a large storm drain behind the only McDonald's on our side of Pittsburgh. A hundred feet into it I started to worry about the stream of water we had to straddle, the stains on the inside of the pipe that showed water, at least once, had reached more than halfway up the sides, enough to flush us out, drowned along the way.

It was raining outside. If it suddenly fell harder, maybe things would add up to the sort of flash flood that swept away thirteen-year-old fools. We worked our way to a sort of intersection, and I followed Charlie and Dave up the ladder to where Charlie popped up the manhole cover that turned out to be near Gimbel's, the department store that anchored the shopping center next to McDonald's.

"Maybe Jack Hall will put a pipe like this under his shelter now," Charlie said. "And then we could pop up inside after the war starts and make ourselves at home. He couldn't open the door to throw us out."

"Fat chance," I said, but what we all agreed on was we needed guns. We watched television shows depicting the dilemma of admitting neighbors and diminishing the chances of survival. Even so, we all knew nobody would actually finish a bomb shelter except fanatics like Jack Hall. "Two days after the blast," the civil defense manual said, "only one-percent of radioactivity is left, but the radiation may be so intense at the start that one-percent may be extremely dangerous."

"When does the last one-percent go away?" I asked my father, and he spread his arms as if he was describing the world's largest fish-that-got-away.

That summer Pennsylvania was invaded by tent caterpillars. Trees sprouted gauzy nests that promised disaster, and those caterpillars had dozens of nests on the crabapple tree by Charlie's driveway. I looked into the nests where, through the web-like covering, I could see hundreds of thin caterpillars swarming as if they wanted to break out and get to work on the leaves of that tree or my body if I was foolish enough to let them cover me. "It's creepy how you can see right inside these things," Charlie said.

"They're translucent," I said, remembering the word from my eighth-grade science class and the quiz on *transparent*, *translucent*, and *opaque*.

"The better to see them burn," Charlie said, lugging a gallon can of gasoline out of his father's garage. "Let's nuke them. Let's do Hiroshima on as many as we can."

The caterpillars were hideous. I had no trouble finding a stick and helping Charlie lift cocoons from the tree and drop them into a puddle of gasoline he'd poured into a low spot where his driveway widened near a small pipe that took run-off water away from the garage. Most of the nests stuck to our sticks when we nudged the ends of them, and if they didn't, the caterpillars spilling out as we walked them to the puddle, we stepped on as many as we could.

When we had ten of those nests in place, it seemed as if there were thousands of caterpillars, most of them still inside their translucent houses. Fumes from the gasoline Charlie had poured rose around us as we leaned over to look. The mouth of the pipe looked hazy. "This stuff is like dope," Charlie said. "People sniff this to get like they're drunk."

I nodded. Charlie's father, according to mine, "liked his drink," but no one in my house drank, so I had no idea what it was to "get like they're drunk."

I took a step back and then another as Charlie splashed more gasoline on the mess. He leaned back down and scraped one of his big wooden matches that lit when scraped across any rough surface. A cloud of flame blew up so close to his face he arced back like a gymnast, sprawling among the loose caterpillars as the flame roiled for a second or two and then sucked back down to campfire size.

"Shit," he said. "Holy shit," and his hands went to his face, resting on his cheeks and then his forehead like my mother's did when she tested me for fever.

I shook a caterpillar off my shoe. "That was close," he said, laughing, getting up and leaning over to look at the roasted worms. "Look at them all," he said, "the dumb shits."

Already, the fire was nearly out. The caterpillars looked like the snakes we lit on the 4th of July, only way thinner.

Nobody knew what they were made out of, but we loved the picture of a coiled cobra on the box, and every summer we bought packages of them, lighting the dark, thick pills and watching as dark, gray snakes emerged, curling up, getting longer until they started to collapse on themselves while the stump from which they'd issued hissed and spit and then went quiet.

"They're totaled," Charlie said. "The little shits."

Jack Hall told us Shot Hood was seventy-four kilotons. "You betcha that one was big," he said. "Hiroshima was thirteen. You boys can do the math."

And we did. And we were reading all about bombs, discovering to our delight, a description of the excrement bomb of ancient China. In his *Military Encyclopedia*, 1044, Tseng Kung-Liang gives his recipe:

15 pounds of human excrement—dried, sifted, and powdered
8 ounces wolfsbane
8 ounces aconite
8 ounces croton oil
8 ounces soap-bean pods
8 ounces arsenious oxide
8 ounces arsenic sulfide
4 ounces cantharides beetles
16 ounces ashes
8 ounces tung oil

All of this wonderful mess was mixed with gunpowder and catapulted into the enemy where it was supposed to irritate the skin and raise blisters. The ingredients were mysterious enough for us to believe that those blisters would cover some enemy's body and cause him unendurable agony. In the book we read, it said the artillerymen who fired those bombs were told to suck black plums and eat licorice to protect themselves.

"Fat chance that would work," Dave Tolley said, but already we had decided to add ashes and lima bean pods and hot pepper when we made our next dog shit assault.

Nothing looked different as the bag burned, but this time, at last, one man stomped on the fire and then ran directly at us. At ten o'clock, Friday night, he was wearing a white shirt and a tie, deserving shit on his shoes for sporting a costume like that so late. And though all three of us wanted to bolt, we knew his accurate direction was an accident, that if we stayed behind the thick, fat junipers across the street from his house, we could watch him slow down when he reached the asphalt, then stop and scream again, adding, "I know you're out here" to every scatological expletive as if hearing him would make us reconsider the deployment of shit.

Life magazine published "Their Sheltered Honeymoon" during August, the Minisons smiling for the cameras as if a bomb shelter was a swell place to start a marriage, the three of us joking about how they must have had the world's greatest honeymoon because there wasn't anything else to do but have sex. Kruschev, declaring more Communist technological advances, had told Nixon, "When we catch you up, in passing you by, we will wave to you."

"The world doesn't seem to know itself, Gary," Jack Hall told me one afternoon before I met up with Dave and Charlie. "You march toward Ground Zero and everything clears up in a hurry. There's nothing at all to worry about except the next step and then the next and the next after that. Everything else is gone. Vanished. Vamoosed."

I nodded, thinking of the desert and tumbleweeds, the sheriff in a hundred movies showing his deputies where the outlaws have gotten to. "You'll see when the time comes," Jack Hall said finally. "Your old man ought to get his ass in gear. He's got a family worth saving, and he's out mowing his lawn."

When school started, our social studies teacher gave us a problem to solve:

A bomb shelter can hold eight people long enough for them to survive World War III. However, there are sixteen people inside, and we have to choose, in the thirty minutes before the missiles arrive, which eight will get to live and which eight will get pushed out into the holocaust.

We threw out the politician, the lawyer, and the minister. We were ninth graders now, so we shoved the teacher outside. It didn't take long to add the artist and the soldier, taking for granted that we had the guns, not him. Finally, we evicted the two people who were over fifty years old.

Who did we keep? Inside, waiting out the years until that lethal one-percent dissipated, were two teenagers (a boy and a girl), the engineer, and the survivalist. Besides them, we kept two small children, a carpenter, and a mechanic. They were good choices, nearly everyone agreed. Only the engineer wore a tie to work, and he could be persuaded, we thought, to never wear it again.

ANTHROPOLOGY

BY JENNY HANNING

A sure determination of your value:

When your estrangement ends
Go through your mother's underwear drawer
And see how many envelopes
Of your hair she kept.

TREE ROOTS

BY YELIZAVETA P. RENFRO

It is Natalie's idea to dig up the root that sticks up like a broken-off splinter from the middle of our front yard, and even though the temperature hovers around ninety with a matching ninety percent humidity, I go along. The heat, the humidity, the glaring afternoon sun impaled in the middle of the July-blue sky like a shiny nail head: these are all part of our punishment. At least it means Natalie is not, for now, the milk-faced ghost that floats through the rooms of our house. She decorously chips away at the ground with a shovel, half-hearted in her effort. It is symbolic for her, this act. I swing the pick-axe hard, up over my head and down, up and down, throwing up fresh black clods of earth. They rain down on the matted lawn, black eyes glaring up at the sky. The sweat-ants crawl down my back, and I swing again, and again. Here we are, husband and wife, working side by side. Everything is right, for now.

The root is tenacious, clutching the ground as though unaware that its reason for being—the tree it nourished—is gone, six months gone, more than six months gone. It clings for no reason. I tear at its tentacles, refusing to find any symbolism in any of this. Symbolism is for the sentimental. The white pine fell in a storm back in late December. There it was one morning, snapped at the trunk, its mealy yellow flesh showing through the jagged break. Upon inspection, I discovered that the borers had gotten it. Its core was mottled with their tiny passageways. I should have known. I know about trees. But this one was green and lush until the day it cracked in two. I cut up the dead tree for firewood, leaving the root in the frozen ground until the spring thaw. In the meantime, I began to plan for a replacement: a fast-growing shade tree, large, stately, with high, strong branches.

Natalie pauses to dab at her temples with the back of her hand. She is wearing a purple bandana on her head. Tendrils of dark hair coil on her neck. When I look at her for too long, she goes back to work, leaning her weight on the shovel with an expression of intense concentration. It was almost a year ago, on a day very much like this one, a steamy July day, the very pith of summer, moist and bright, when she sweated and toiled in that hospital room. I push my body harder, pushing away thoughts, swinging the axe.

Suddenly, we find our rhythm, and we begin to work in synch. Natalie is really shoveling now, pushing hard, digging deep. It's no longer for show. The supple muscles of Natalie's arms work in perfect counterpoint to my own: swing-*hrussh*, shovel-*thack*, swing-*hrussh*, shovel-*thack*. A pile of chipped-off root fragments grows between us. We are accomplishing something, Natalie and I. We are making this pile, this hole.

"There she is," Natalie suddenly hisses, tossing a look behind my back. She pauses, leaning her weight on the shovel, staring into our shared hole.

I feel it behind me: the Kelson house, and all that it has come to mean in the last year—no, fifteen months. We have learned to count things first in days, then weeks, and now months. I turn around, and there, standing in the center of her smooth, green lawn is Chelsea Kelson, looking at me with a smirk, triumphant that yet another tree will be gone from the neighborhood. If she had it her way, there would be no trees in the world, what with their messy leaf detritus, their dangerous falling branches, their ungainliness, their imperfection. The world would be made of flat, smooth, safe, easy-to-mow lawns. The anger begins to burn again low in my stomach.

"Why didn't she move out to suburbia?" I mutter to Natalie. "Out to one of those new treeless developments with plastic houses and manufactured lawns. One of those places where you have to get permission to plant so much as a daisy in your own yard."

"Stop it," Natalie says flatly. "Just ignore her." She plunges her shovel back into the ground. I look at her face and see the strain around her eyes. I go back to work, but we've lost our rhythm. I think of my beautiful doomed trees and nearly choke on my anger.

"Co-sleeping might reduce the risk of SIDS." Natalie makes this announcement coolly, a smooth punch. She pauses to wipe sweat from her forehead with the back of her hand.

"It has to do with an adult's breathing helping to regulate the infant's breathing," she continues calmly, her eyes on me.

"Natalie," I say.

"I know. It doesn't matter," she says. "But I am her *mother*. I will *always* be her mother." She abruptly abandons her shovel in the dirt and heads for the house.

I throw myself back into digging up that root. The hole has sprawled out in every direction, tentacle trenches radiating from the center pit, as though a giant starfish exploded up from the ground.

Natalie is sitting at the computer. I can see her through the window, even though I don't want to see her. The monitor's light brims milk-blue on her face hanging there like a sad moon. I know what she is doing, with her online support groups, her e-mail networks, her scouring of the web for any new article, any shred of new fact to cling to. I know what she is doing, going over the story in her mind again and again, remaking it. I will not participate, because there is nothing to extract from the events, no truth or meaning, nothing at the empty core of it.

I am usually not an angry person, and so it angers me that Chelsea Kelson has made me so angry. Being a bus driver, I've gotten used to people's impetuous behavior. I take it all in stride: the crazy, battered people who ride my bus, the distracted lawyers, shoppers, mothers out on the road who are lawyers, shoppers, mothers first and drivers only second. If you take it personally, you'll end up with an ulcer or a heart attack. I'm a cool, rational machine, sitting up there above the rest of the world, operating my bus with clean precision, removed from the messy emotion that pours out of everyone else. I'm a driver first and foremost.

I try to keep working, gouging at the root, but I can see her, standing there, smug as you please, that tree-hater. She is watching me, waiting for something, but I ignore her. Finally she starts to walk in my direction, stopping with her feet edging over my property line. I say nothing and chop away at the ground.

"Just so you know, the workers are coming back tomorrow," she says loudly.

I gouge on, blind, unable to see what I'm tearing: earth, root, lawn?

"Just try to call the police again," she challenges. "Just try it."

I turn my back to her and work on.

"I've instructed my workers," she calls out. "They know the police can't do anything. They know to keep working, no matter what."

I grab the shovel that Natalie left behind and toss a load of loose dirt in the tree-hater's direction, but it falls short of her manicured toes, still wiggling over my property line. I imagine lopping them off with my axe. I dislike myself for thinking this; I dislike Chelsea Kelson even more for making me think it.

"The work is going to be done, and there's nothing you can do to stop it," she says. "Just accept it." She begins to stride away from me, across her empty lawn, to her house.

"You'll be hearing from my lawyer," I call out, impressed at the impersonal calmness of my voice. I watch her take a slight misstep, then keep walking. Chelsea disappears into her house, the door slamming behind her.

"Why did you move here, to this old neighborhood, with the old stately trees, if you're a tree-hater?" I mutter to myself. "That's what I want to know."

We bought our house, Natalie and I, eight years ago when we married because she loved the old 1922 prairie foursquare, and I loved the old trees: the silver maple, the water birch, the hackberry, the quaking aspen, the pin oak, the Kentucky coffeetree, and the three American elms that grow in the back along the property line. Our old neighbors, the Birdwells, were good people. We would have a beer now and then, sometimes on our porch, sometimes on theirs. They were like us. They appreciated old things and trees.

The trouble started fifteen months ago, when the Birdwells moved to Omaha, and Chelsea Kelson and her two daughters moved into their house. First, she had the trees in her own yard removed, every one of them, and then she set her sights on my trees. Most of them she couldn't touch, but the elms that grow along her property line she thought were fair game. She demanded that the branches that hang over her yard be trimmed, as they posed a danger to her daughters. A branch might fall and kill one of them. This was her line of argument. Back then, I still believed that she was a rational person, so I patiently explained that clear-cutting them was sure to kill them. I even called in a certified arborist to deliver the same opinion. I agreed to have the branches thinned, the dead growth removed. She agreed to the pruning, which cost me half a grand, but afterwards, she said not enough had been taken off. She went back to her original demand: clear-cut the trees at the property line. I refused.

There were some shenanigans on her part when she tried to hire some workers herself to do the work, but then in the late fall and winter months, Chelsea seemed to go dormant along with the trees. They no longer interested her. Before buying the house, she had been through a bad divorce. She was an angry woman, and I was a stand-in for her ex-husband. He wasn't around to hate, so she hated me, and she hated trees. I thought that the anger was going out of her. And after Abby, she backed off completely. I thought she'd given up, but something must have happened with the ex. Now that the trees are at the peak of their summer foliage, she's started in again on her crusade to kill them.

On Friday, a new crew arrived, so I went over to find out what they were up to and learned that they'd been hired to dig a three-foot-deep trench along the property line, cutting off any tree roots they came across. Easily a third if not half of my trees' feeder roots go across Chelsea's property;

cutting them off will kill the trees. I told the workers that they were to do no work and that I was calling the police.

The police did nothing, of course. They told me I could try to get a restraining order, but that would take time. Still, the workers were intimidated by the two cops being there at all. Chelsea was at work, and unable to reach her, they agreed to stop for the day. If they're coming back tomorrow, Chelsea has gotten to them. Or she's hired a new crew. There's no shortage of people willing to destroy things for low wages.

I walk into my backyard and look up at the bursting green tangles of elm branches. They have all grown together, these three trees. Their lives are all knotted up in one another. I touch the trunk of the middle one, warm like flesh in the hot July day. Goodbye, tree. There's nothing I can do. I want to mean the words, but I don't. I want to be resigned to this, to loosen the tight clench I have on my anger, but I can't. Goodbye. For now, goodbye. I lean against the warm trunk of the center tree, allowing it to support my weight.

I don't want to keep hating Chelsea Kelson; I don't want all of my energy to feed that hate. She's not an evil woman, only an angry one. Back in January, after hearing, she came to our house, stood at our door, stammered.

"I'm so sorry about Abby. I would die if that happened to me."

Though I appreciated her gesture, I had no words to return. I could only think of her standing in her yard, her healthy, beautiful daughters flanking her; Jenna the blonde, Lila the brunette. I wanted to explain it to her. You would not die, I wanted to say. It's like this: it's now, you see, and right now, I can stand it. And later, it will be now, and I will still stand it, but just for now. I did not say these things. I said, "Thank you." I said, "I will tell Natalie you were here."

But I did not tell Natalie, because she was so far away from everything that it would have meant nothing at all to her. It would have been like words in a foreign language shouted at a shipwreck survivor from a passing yacht. She used to say that I was a wonderful father. She never says it anymore. She is a mother forever; the child came out of her. I am nothing, a ghost. My connection to everything is tenuous. Natalie suffers in her mind, in her heart, in her womb. I am the white-haired ghost with the ghostly grief, leaning on a tree.

"Hiya, old man," says Bill, boarding my bus.

"Hi yourself, old man," I answer back, because this is what we say, Bill and I. He sits behind me, as always, but he doesn't say more. There's nothing to say. There's only the old joke between us that somehow won't die. We're the same age; in actual fact, Bill is a few months older, but while my hair is all white and has been for years, Bill's is brown. We both came to fatherhood late, Bill and I. Bill has a two-year-old son, Max, but we don't talk about him anymore. He must be almost three by now.

I'm three minutes ahead of schedule, so we sit, here at 22nd and Smith. Just five blocks to the northwest is my house, where my trees are being killed. I want to punch the gas, be out of here, but I still have two minutes. I haven't closed the doors, so I can feel the waves of heat come licking in against my arms, chilled from the air conditioning.

"How's that boy of yours?" I say, and it comes out mean-sounding, like a curse.

Bill pauses for a long time. "Great," he finally says, but not like he means it. There's just no right answer to that question.

"Great," I say, and I know that's all we're going to say.

I never intended to become a bus driver. I just backed into it, after running a landscaping business, then working in an office, doing payroll at the university. One day I saw an ad in the paper: bus drivers wanted, no experience necessary, good pay and benefits. I thought, why not? I could get out, see things, talk to people. I would try it for a while, until something else came along. I've been doing it now for sixteen years. As I grew older, I learned to commit to things: to my job, to Natalie. It took me longer than some to commit. I was forty when we married.

I used to like it that driving a bus wasn't mentally taxing, once you knew what you were doing. I could do it with one part of my mind while I thought of Natalie and Abby with the other. And then, I could be really there for them when I came home—not tired and distant, the way that people who do mental work all day are. But then for a little while after Abby, I thought I couldn't bear this job anymore, with all this freedom for the mind to rove. I wanted to have the kind of job that robbed you of all your energy, physical and mental. And then I found a way to be at peace with it. It's simple: now, this section of my life is my time with Abby. The rest of the time, I live without her. It's easier to compartmentalize this way.

So I let my thoughts drift to her, to the feel of her in my arms, her warm sleeping puddle shape, breathing, and her gummy greedy starfish hands, grabbing, leeching to my fingers, my nose, my ears, my collar. I remember her tender infant eyes that would catch, for an instant, on the shimmering leaves of the quaking aspen, and suddenly I thought the world of that tree because she had looked at it. I would strap her to my chest and carry her around the neighborhood, showing her off to anyone who cared to look. Sometimes people mistook me for her grandfather, or they just weren't sure, but I didn't care, not with Abby tucked up against me.

She was the only one. There will be no more. I am forty-eight, Natalie forty-two. There were three miscarriages before Abby. Maybe we were too old. The medical examiner said that sometimes there's an undetectable and fatal defect that they could not find. But for that, she was perfection.

At the main terminal downtown, the passengers churn to life, gathering up bags to make connections, to rush off to appointments. Bill gives me a quick nod on his way out. I wait, looking at nothing, while new passengers begin to come on. I used to think about who they were, but I don't anymore. They're all the same. There are the ones that strike up a conversation; the ones that are crazy, drunk, or stoned; the ones that don't speak English; the ones that don't want to pay; the ones with sob stories; the ones that are normal; the ones that vomit on the bus; the ones that forget their cell phones, purses, books, newspapers, briefcases, duffel bags, Ipods, Gameboys, glasses, hats, umbrellas, gloves, or toys; the ones that spill soda; the children; the ones that talk to themselves; the ones that talk to everyone else; the ones that tell me how to drive; the ones that curse at motorists; the ones that are late; the furtive ones; the loud ones; the terrified ones; the terrifying ones; the ones in wheelchairs; the limping ones; the sad ones; the blind; the sick; and the angry ones.

I pull away from the curb, beginning again the outbound journey. Abby is not very strong with me today. The tree-hater has poisoned my thoughts. I keep returning to my trees, being murdered. I try to think of something calming. I think of being at home, of puttering around the tool shed. And then I remember that there, hanging on a hook on the wall, is the set of miniature plastic garden tools: a red rake, a yellow shovel, a purple hoe. Obscenely bright and clean, they are still packaged together with their original label and pricetag. Each time I enter the shed, they punish me again, unused, untouched. I got them because I am a gardener, because I wanted her to love what I loved, because I wanted an attentive little creature to follow me around the yard, interested in everything I did, curious, because I wanted to teach her everything I knew. Those tools should be dirty and loved and scattered. A grungy plastic rake should lie bleaching in the sun beside the yew.

I have just one more run after this one. Then my time with Abby will be over for today. I will go home to look at the damage wrought by a woman with her misdirected anger. Destroying my property, hating me, turning her daughters against me like I'm some kind of a sex offender. I can imagine what she says to them. Stay away from that man. He's dangerous, he's angry, he's volatile, he wants tree branches to fall on your head. The older one, Jenna, stares me down with a glare as mean as her mother's. Lila, the younger one, hasn't gotten it yet. She still flashes her gap-toothed grin at me. She is still innocent. But not for long, not with a mother like that. For a while I had naively thought that there would be a way for us to work things out, two reasonable neighbors. And then there was that day in spring, one of the first warm, bud-and-shoot-filled days, when Chelsea said the one unforgivable thing: "Don't take your daughter's death out on me."

"It's all over," Natalie says to me from where she is perched at her computer. I close the door behind me, shutting out the wall of heat. She sits placidly, staring at the blue glow of her monitor, huddled there in the chill of the air conditioning in a gray sweatshirt. The Natalie who got up and did things—the fierce Natalie of yesterday, tearing at the tree root—has retreated. The cool, moonlike Natalie is back.

"And you sat in here all day, and you did nothing," I finally say.

"There was nothing I could do."

"Time to find a lawyer."

"Time to forget about it," Natalie says, turning to look at me. "Forget about the trees, forget about the lawyer. Enough already."

"She killed my trees, Natalie. I have to hire a lawyer. I have to."

"No, you don't. You don't have to do a thing." She looks back at the computer.

"*You* don't have to do a thing."

"What does that mean?" she asks sharply.

"Natalie, I can't just let this pass."

"I don't care about those trees, OK?"

"Someone has to care about something."

"You're saying that to *me*?" She glares at me, her index finger poised at her chest. *Me*, it points, a *mother*.

"Natalie."

"Nobody can own a tree," she says, her moon-voice back. "You don't own it, she doesn't own it."

"She's killing them."

"They'll die anyway." Her voice is impersonal, like that of someone from up on high, the voice of wisdom.

"Nobody owns a life," I say. "Isn't that what you really mean? Nobody controls a life. Nobody can save a life. Not even a parent, not even a *mother*."

I want to say: It doesn't matter how or why it happened. It doesn't matter because we will never know. It doesn't matter because Abby is gone. *And that is all that matters.* But I don't. I let the barb of the word *mother* sink in. All the words we've exchanged, all the events that did happen and might have happened and could and should have happened: they are like ticks in Natalie's mind, preying upon her, each one becoming engorged with her obsession, her hurt, and I cannot extract, I cannot kill them.

"I'd rather remember her the way she was, the time we had with her," I finally say, leaving the rest unspoken. But Natalie is clever; she picks up on the unsaid, another tick. She doesn't reply, and I am tired. I just can't do it right now. I can't love her enough to say more, to give her even an ounce of energy, when she gives nothing back.

I look around the living room as though some object is going to help me through this, but I see nothing at all that means anything. Sofas, chairs, a TV, our stuff. I see nothing. And I realize that the room looks as though no child has ever lived here. All of Abby's things are now sealed off in the shrine that Natalie has made of the nursery, a room I find no reason to enter. I open my mouth to say something, but Natalie is already hammering away at the keys on her computer.

So I close my mouth and walk to the kitchen to look for some dinner, even though I'm not hungry. Instead, I look out the back window at my elms, which from this vantage point look green and healthy as ever, but for that new raw gash of earth along the property line that I can just make out. I stand and look at the trees for a long time, not really thinking anything at all. I have to go out and survey the damage, but I want to put it off as long as I can.

Returning to the living room, I find Natalie asleep on the sofa, her eyebrows twisted into a scowl. Even in sleep, the ticks prey at her mind. I want to pick them out, one by one. I look at my wife and can read the thoughts roiling within her as well as if they were my own: *But she napped fine. And that was after she hit her head. But what if the blood seeped slowly, insidiously around her brain in a deadly pool? But the medical examiner said: no sign of head trauma, no sign of anything. It was a cold night, and there was the extra blanket. And she had recently learned to turn over. She had turned over that night, onto her stomach, the deadly position. She hit her head, it was cold, there was an extra blanket, she was on her stomach: so many risk factors. No wonder, no wonder. When they found nothing wrong, they called it SIDS. A catch-all term, meaning: we don't know. Meaning: all that is mysterious, beyond the reach of science. Meaning: why was our baby taken from us? Meaning: this is the worst thing that can ever happen to a mother.*

I sense it all, swirling in her mind, even in sleep. On top of the guilt, there was the suspicion: You let her hit her head. You covered her with that blanket. These silent accusations always hang between us. But it doesn't matter, it doesn't matter, it doesn't matter: I direct this at my sleeping wife. Yes, she hit her head under Natalie's watch. But she was fine. She napped and woke up and nursed and did all the things a baby should do. Yes, I put an extra blanket on her that night. It doesn't matter. It doesn't matter. I learned this, and Natalie did not. Her mind did not, and her body did not. The weeping hard melons of her breasts leaked milk for days, coming through even the pads, crying too for their loss. You have to drink, I told her. You will dehydrate. She pulled away, angered that I could have such a mundane idea at this time, angered that I wanted to deny her the denial of her body. Her body made this child; her body must suffer the loss of this child. She pulled away then, and she continues to pull away, hiding behind the shield of the holy word *mother*.

For no particular reason, I sit down in Natalie's computer chair and glance at the screen. A browser window is open with a page from a medical site. I begin to read.

Infants who succumb to SIDS may have an abnormality in the arcuate nucleus, a part of the brain that may help control breathing and awakening during sleep. If a baby is breathing stale air and not getting enough oxygen, the brain usually triggers the baby to wake up and cry. That movement changes the breathing and heart rate, making up for the lack of oxygen. But a problem with the arcuate nucleus could deprive the baby of this involuntary reaction and put him or her at greater risk for SIDS.

I notice that other programs are open, minimized at the bottom of the screen. I click on the first one, bringing up an e-mail.

Honey, only another mother who's gone through it can understand. The hurt cuts deep like a knife and never goes away, never, no matter what other people say. It goes on cutting and cutting forever. And it should. Don't ever let it stop. Remember your angel forever, keep her in your heart forever.

Elaina, mommy of little angel Trenton Zachary Matthias Dunn, April 14, 1997-June 2, 1997

I click on another file at the bottom of the screen, bringing up a window of text.

I've posted my story here before, so I won't repeat all of those painful details. Today I am creating a celebration of my angel's life because today is a milestone. My angel Abby lived 5 months, 27 days. I have now lived 5 months, 27 days without her.

born July 23, 2005—died January 19, 2006—today is July 16, 2006.

Today I pass this milestone. Every day from now on I get farther and farther from my angel. Every day the time without her grows, making her short life shrink. What will it be like when I say it's been 10 years without Abby, and only 5 months, 27 days with her? I will not let her shrink. In a week she will be one. Exactly one week from today, at 9:09 p.m. Happy Birthday, Abby, mommy's little angel.

I feel a physical recoil from the words that makes me get up from the computer. The words don't reach me at all. They are sentimental, mawkish. It's like they were written by someone I don't know, someone I don't want to know.

Before I realize what I'm doing, I'm headed up the stairs, and I think: *Good. I will change out of my uniform. I will go outside to look at the trees.* The thoughts are clear, rational. In our bedroom, I stop to look down over Chelsea's backyard, and in the fading light I can see that Chelsea and Jenna are crouched over, coloring with chalk on their cement patio. For a moment, they're just that: a mother and daughter, innocently coloring with chalk. I almost feel a flash of forgiveness, seeing them that way, but then they both stand up at the same time and walk over to the edge to survey their work. And then I see what they have done: in large, multi-colored letters, angled so that I can read them perfectly from my window, they have written me a message.

> *God grant me the serenity*
> *to accept the things I cannot change*
> *the courage to change the things I can*
> *and the wisdom to know the difference*

My eyes travel over the words three times before I understand what they mean, and then anger washes over me, the magnitude of it stupefying, like some near-fatal attack on the body, or like grief.

I look into the deep trench, hiding in its shadows the sawed-off roots, invisibly bleeding out the life of my trees. Somewhere in the distance I hear a child's repetitive chant, three lines and then a refrain, three lines and a refrain. I can't make out the words. There is nothing for me to do here. The deed is done. I touch the bark of each elm as I walk past, into the front yard. I stop for a moment at the hole Natalie and I dug yesterday, at our unfinished labor sprawling here on the lawn. Our front yard, torn open, bare, seems to have no future. I can usually envision a dozen landscape possibilities for any yard, but here I see nothing. And then, briefly, I glimpse a supple, strong tree that doesn't grow here, a swing that doesn't hang from a branch, a girl that doesn't ride in the swing. And then I erase it from my mind because I will not be sentimental. I am not that way.

Suddenly I feel a presence behind my back. My mind fills with angry words, but when I turn, I see that it is only Lila Kelson, drawing with chalk at the end of her driveway. I don't want to look at what she's doing; I don't want to know what her mother and sister have put her up to. So without any real plan, I end up crossing the street to get away from the Kelson house. And then I am strolling, heading for the end of the block, the way I used to every day, with Abby, but my hands are empty. They feel large, obscene, hanging at my sides like useless rudders. I get to the end of the block, and then I keep going.

People are out in their yards, enjoying the summer evening that is still bursting with warmth and light. At one house I see a teenaged boy strumming a guitar on the porch. At another, a boy climbs out of a second-floor window onto the porch roof to talk on his cell phone. This is not so bad, I think. This is almost living. Fireflies hang in the sticky humid air like lights suspended in twilight-colored liquid, and all the neighborhood, all the city, seems suspended in the summer, trapped in this jar of here, of now. And it is always now, always now.

As I turn a corner, I realize that all of this time I've been headed in the direction of the chanting, which has continued and grown louder. And now I can make out the words: "God's eyes for sale! God's eyes for sale! God's eyes for sale! And a person!" a girl cries with great gusto. There is a pause, and then she begins again: "God's eyes for sale! God's eyes for sale! God's eyes for sale! And a person!"

I find her perched on a small front stoop, a collection of the yarn-and-popsicle-stick, diamond-shaped crafts known as God's eyes spread out around her on the cement. As she chants, she is busy at work, yarn flying through nimble fingers. When I approach her, she glances up at me just long enough to take me in, then looks back at her project.

"Hey, bus driver," she says. "Wanna buy some God's eyes?"

I look down at the uniform I've forgotten to change out of. "They're beautiful," I say. "But I don't have any money. Will you be here tomorrow?"

"Maybe, maybe not," she replies out of the corner of her mouth as she performs a complicated maneuver with the sticks and yarn. She doesn't want to make any promises. She clearly wants to make a sale today, but my pockets are empty. I finger them, pushing at the seams. Nothing.

"Let me take a look at that person," I say. She surveys the work spread out around her, plucking up one of her wares and handing it to me. I turn it over in my hand, carefully examining the popsicle stick head, arms, and legs, inexpertly tied together with red yarn.

"That was the hardest to make," she boasts.

"I'll come back for it tomorrow," I promise.

"It's the only one I have," she warns. "That's why it's $2.50. The God's eyes are $1 each."

I hand the person back to her, and turn to head home. When I reach the corner, she picks up her singsong pitch once again. "God's eyes for sale! God's eyes for sale! God's eyes for sale! And a person!"

When I get back to my block, I see that there's no one in the Kelson yard. I approach the driveway where Lila worked, dreading to see the message she's left me. The light is beginning to fail, but I can immediately make out the single word she has written in the driveway, in an exuberant splendor of pink and lavender bubble letters, each one filled to bursting with balloons, butterflies, flowers, stars, and hearts. The word is LOVE.

For a moment, I step out of the roiling world into stillness. For now, for now, my heart beats out, as I look at the chalked letters, I let go of my anger, and I let myself imagine that two hearts are beating in my house, Abby's and Natalie's, that they are both there, sleeping, waiting for tomorrow, breathing in and out, for now, for now, and I wish that when I had them both, for those five months, twenty-seven days, I had stood here, just like this, loving them with each beat of my own heart, for now, for now, grateful for what I had, perfectly serene. I can hear the rapid, precarious thud-thud-thud of my daughter's tiny heart: for now, for now, for now. I would do anything to bring back Abby. I can't say the same of Natalie.

I look up at my house, past the tentacled black hole with the half-excavated root, at the darkened windows, like eyes that have burned out their life. And then I look past all of that, above the house, at the snarled blot of ripe summer green, my elms still towering there, for now, for now.

LEDA AND THE SWANS

BY MARY HELEN SPECHT

The swans were nesting that year on Town Lake. When this happens, the city puts up a makeshift fence around their enormous mound of laced twigs and debris, candy wrappers and mysterious fuzz, with a sign that says "ATTENTION: Nesting Swans. Do Not Disturb," and people stroll by on their lunch break or after work in the hopes of getting lucky, in the hopes of seeing the cygnets hatch or at least soon after, gummy and pink and half-blind. The swan-parents-to-be crane their long necks in casual indifference at the passersby. There are updates in the newspaper and bets made in break rooms; children say, "Did you sit on me, mommy? To keep me warm?"

Leda and her fiancé Adam started going early in the morning with their tea in matching insulated travel mugs to squat beside the fluffed-up birds and project peaceful thoughts to the sleeping pile of feathers. Leda knew, possessing a name inspired by the Greek legend, that her passion for swans was both predictable and melodramatic. She didn't care. They were stunning.

"He never seems to leave her side," she said, on day three of the swan watch. "They're a very modern couple. Partners."

"I'm not leaving you, Leda. We're doing this together."

"Oh, I know, I know. I was just saying is all. About them." Leda and Adam stood there for a few moments in silence until she said, "I'm not going."

"What do you mean?"

"I'm staying here with the swans."

And so Adam moved to New York for the "once-in-a-lifetime" opportunity to work slave hours for slave wages at the firm of the "starchitect" where he'd been hired. And Leda moved into a boarding house in a different part of Austin and continued to work as a Young Adult librarian at the Terrazas branch in east Austin. The wedding was still on, Leda assured him, she just needed time to put things in order. She was in the middle of a literacy project; she hadn't yet applied for any jobs there; his hiring straight out of grad school had just come so fast; she wasn't ready. This is what she told him, and it was true. But there was also something else, something she couldn't have explained even if she'd wanted to, a feeling that she just needed to sit somewhere quiet for a while.

The boarding house was north of Anderson Lane in a neighborhood full of transplanted techies, much too far to make the walk past the swans each morning. But she moved there because it wasn't financially feasible for them to pay for two entire apartments and also so she wouldn't be tied into a lease and could move up to New York as soon as things were settled.

One might imagine there would be a camaraderie among roommates, but these days anyway, people who live in boarding houses instinctively learn to listen from their doorways before padding down to the bathroom or kitchen so as to avoid bumping into each other unnecessarily. People who live in boarding houses do not want to be asked questions. Her first morning in the house, Leda awoke to the sound of the other woman who lived on her floor crying. Someone must have died, she thought, because in the hall outside the woman's door sat a cardboard box piled high with sick person things: a pink plastic bedpan, a tangle of IV tubes, an afghan crusted with some awful dried bodily fluid. Don't ask, Leda thought to herself, just don't ask.

Adam called almost every night, and sometimes she picked up the phone. He bitched about the job, the long hours and tedious work. This was nothing new. Even during graduate school, he'd often told people she was an architect's widow as if they would automatically understand what that meant or as if it were funny.

"When? Please, just give me a date so I'll have *something*," he would say.

"Soon. I've sent out a few applications."

"I want a date."

"You are not calling the shots here."

Leda met Russell two days after her move at a housewarming party thrown by a close friend. Angélica's was a beautiful apartment. She'd splurged on it after winning a small journalism prize, but, in all honesty, she couldn't really afford to rent a place so large in a building with such detail: crown molding, Spanish tile, a whirlpool. The shop on the first floor sold more kinds of gelato than Leda knew existed. Angélica had obviously tried to downplay the snooty elegance of the place by playing flamenco music and lighting sandalwood incense and draping scarves over the windows—red with big white cherry blossoms. She was plump, with frizzy black hair, but she pulled it off; she dressed to accentuate her curves, in tunics that made her all breasts and hips, and pinned her hair up loosely so it escaped in wild tufts and so it set off the ovalness of her face.

They had met in college, both waiting tables part-time at the same anglicized Mexican restaurant with strings of chili-pepper lights hanging from the ceiling, and Angélica was even the one who introduced her to Adam and who would be the maid of honor in the wedding for which they had yet to set a date. But Leda was always the practical one, The General they called her, the one who knew what to look for in an apartment, in a checking account, and where to get pants altered and how to get blood out of underwear and bake pot brownies and pot scotchies and pot pumpkin pie for Thanksgiving and how to change a tire, jump an engine, complain effectively to credit card companies. Angélica, on the other hand, hated having to deal with any of these details, and she was no good at it anyway; she lost or forgot or ruined everything: keys, purse, phone, Leda's favorite western belt with the buckle in the shape of Texas. She played up her role as resident Free Spirit, skirts worn over pants and her shoulders stooped by so many beads, and for some reason Leda didn't mind; she wasn't really bothered by all the attention Angélica garnered this way. Maybe, although she'd hate to admit it, it was because she possessed the feeling of superiority, however undeserved, that comes with being considered the more attractive friend.

There were a lot of people Leda knew vaguely milling about the party; they were not used to seeing her without Adam. Some of them, especially those she'd met through her fiancé, had become suddenly shy as if expecting her to introduce herself all over again. Most of the guests were more or less her age, which was twenty-nine, but they all seemed to be either perpetual students or boho vagabonds. There was even a boyish-looking woman playing the washboard in the corner. Adam and Leda were the first couple of this particular circle to become engaged.

Russell was a recent convert, one of Angélica's new fast friends: nobody knew how she did it, how she managed to juggle so many intimate friendships with so many different people—and it wasn't as if she were the kind who eventually dropped you to move on to someone else—especially so many men, some of who might have been in love with her but whom she rarely slept with. Russell was in the Land Art class she was taking at the community center. When he and Leda met at the party, he said he was an arborist. He said it was "absolutely horrible" to meet her and, then, that her figure reminded him of an acacia tree. They were both drinking vodka.

"Did you hear about the refrigerator?" he asked, his gleaming bald head shaven as was popular with youngish men losing hair on their crowns, ducking toward her so he could whisper.

"Is this the beginning of a joke?" she asked. "Is this that joke about your refrigerator running and then something about how you better go catch it?"

"No joke. Did you hear what Angélica did to her refrigerator when she moved into this place? They had to evacuate the entire building," he said. He said she'd attempted to defrost the freezer by going at it with an ice pick, eventually puncturing the cavity that held the Freon.

He said the landlord took one look and said, "If I didn't know any better, I'd say someone had stabbed this with an ice pick."

"Can you imagine?" Russell asked. "All these years she's lived alone, and she never learned how to defrost a refrigerator."

"That's what people love about her," Leda replied. "She's the smartest person we know who can't figure out how to open a jar of peanut butter."

Russell told her about the Land Art project he was working on at the Texas State Cemetery. He told her he was exploring the way nature and humans communicated with each other, the ways they tamed each other and shaped each other's behavior and sense of self. Before she could ask him what in the world he was talking about, a woman wearing tight leather pants, from the library where she worked, grabbed her arm and shuffled Leda into a corner by the bookshelf, wanting to know "all the dirt" on why she'd stayed behind in Austin. "And Billy told me you haven't even given your thirty days' notice," the woman said, squinting from behind rectangular fashion glasses.

Leda excused herself politely, saying she had to go to the bathroom, but she actually went out onto the wrought-iron balcony softly lit by paper lanterns for a smoke. A young couple, glistening and slick, were making out in the swimming pool below, but they were wearing clothes, jeans and t-shirts, and the pool was officially closed for the night, so Leda imagined it had been spontaneous; one of them had pushed the other in.

Through the window, she could see Russell speaking animatedly, over-the-top, his gestures hyperbolic; his expressions made her think of the word *tragedian*. He wore a fabulous brown wool suit from a different era that fit as if it had been tailored to his tall blockish body, and maybe it had, and old man brown dress shoes. The thought crossed her mind she had never seen an outfit quite so fabulous outside of photographs, maybe ever. And that's when she knew it was a done deal. As much as it didn't feel like making a decision, as much as it seemed more like watching a wine glass fall from her hands, that was the point when the two of them became inevitable.

"I heart your suit," she said, having cornered him by the tasseled lampshade. "I bet you have a whole closet full of suits like that."

"Thanks. I have a few," he said. "Would you like to see them sometime?"

"What about right now?"

The moment he turned off the ignition, they began kissing the side of each other's faces and necks and running palms over shoulder crevices and chests. In a way, they looked like teenagers parked in front of their parents' house making out in the front seat, but with his bald head and her chenille wrap, they could also have looked like a much older couple; they could easily have looked like an older couple in the frenetic throws of an affair.

Despite what her friends from the North said—complaining the seasons were what they missed most about Pennsylvania or Michigan—Texas did have seasons other than hot and fucking hot. They were just subtle. No blizzards. No fiery spreads of trees the color of blood. But in Austin in the spring, it was light that gave it away. The winter sun, which glances off buildings and parking lots at almost horizontal angles, gives way to vertical beams that look you in the eye but without the beating summer heat that is to come. In the early spring, it is just unadulterated light.

The morning after Leda's first night with Russell was like that, and still in the clothes she'd worn to Angélica's party, she pulled dark sunglasses from her bag and walked along the Shoal Creek path from his house, catty-corner to the hippie bead store on 9th, toward Book People, where she planned to read the paper outside over tea, to browse new Young Adult titles she might order for work, to relax in the sun and enjoy the morning. Then, she would go see the swans. She missed them.

The path was deserted except for the homeless man curled up under the tiny stone bridge and an older woman in a butter-colored jumpsuit coming toward her, walking a Scottish terrier. Just as Leda and the dog began to cross paths, the woman let out a gasp as the terrier suddenly fell over. Like a sleeping cow being tipped, it fell stiffly, as if riger mortis had already set in.

"Is he okay?" Leda asked and the woman said, "Oh god. I think he's dead." The dog opened his eyes and gave what must have been a death rattle before closing them again. There was shit hanging out of his ass, and it was difficult to tell if he was shitting when he died or if dying had caused him to shit.

Leda let the woman use her cell phone to call someone. The woman asked whom she should call and Leda almost said, "Your husband?" but stopped herself and said instead, "The police?" although that didn't seem exactly right either. What could the police do? Arrest the dog reaper? She must have called 911 because Leda heard her say, "It depends on what you mean by an emergency," but eventually she hung up and said the police were on their way.

Typically, Leda was the type who would have stayed with her until they came, smiling comfortingly as the woman choked up telling stories about her now-dead pet. She was the person you wanted with you in a crisis. But it was such a beautiful morning she couldn't bear filling her mood with empathy for another person's loss and said she had to leave. "Wouldn't want the law catching up with me," she said, and, "If they found out about the crimes I've committed, who knows how long they'd lock me up," as if she were kidding, which in a way she was. In a way she wasn't.

Although Leda slept around freshman and sophomore year, Adam had been her first serious boyfriend. After they began dating, she disappeared from her dorm room, basically living at his apartment where the two of them played house. It was like a game in which Adam performed the role of obedient pupil, learning to put the seat down and how to make pasta sauce from scratch. Leda couldn't quite put her finger on the moment it stopped being a choice and became a responsibility; although they waited to get engaged until he finished graduate school, it had always been part of the plan, something they'd whispered about in bed.

One of Leda's biggest disappointments with their extended romantic relationship was how she began to view him along a continuum, to compare him to how he used to be, to not notice how the wrinkles around the eyes softened his face but rather how his countenance had somehow dimmed since she'd first met him nine years earlier. A new lover might appreciate that Adam's brow protruded and gave him an almost sinister air, an air of gloomy sensuality, whereas she looked at him and noticed how his bones seemed to have grown and stretched his features until the perfect boyish symmetry that mocked her in old photographs became unbalanced, occasionally she even thought grotesque, and his constant vigilance and desire to please became patronizing and clingy.

With Russell, she could be the new lover who reached over and caressed the small fold of his belly when he sat down with no shirt on at the breakfast table, and the lover who then said, "That may be the most adorable part of you. But, you know, then again, I just can't seem to decide. Maybe it's here," running a hand down the bends of muscle along his back and shoulder blades, which were sinewy and tough. Russell's job consisted mostly of manual labor mixed in with occasional office work or fundraising for the arboretum where he worked, and his body had the accompanying look, different from the male gym body, trunk-like and solid without the freakishly broad shoulders that come from actual weight-training.

But other than the occasional soil-speckled canvas pants in the hamper, his tiny house betrayed almost nothing of his workaday life. It was almost out of a movie, Leda thought, like out of that silly film where the janitor was really a math genius. Shelves after shelves of hard-bound classics, an ancient Smith-Corona, curtains with weights hand-sewn into the bottom so they hung evenly and no television, no computer; framed black and white photographs of Marxists hung from the wall: his apartment was that of an immaculate aesthete and autodidact and nostalgic. The thought crossed her mind this attention to detail might be a sign he wasn't really into women, or at least not only women, but she later decided it was less the house of an effeminate man than it was one of an old European man, even though Russell was barely thirty and only as European as the affectations he'd absorbed from his books. None of this surprised Leda. She'd always been attracted to decidedly odd men.

"You're ruining the presentation," he said when she wandered groggily into the kitchen—its walls robin-egg blue—one morning before he had finished slicing rich cheeses onto a long rectangular plate. "And you're wearing more clothes than I like to see you in." They ate breakfast with the companionable tenderness and extravagance of new lovers: hand-squeezed tangerine juice, strawberries with real cream, cheese and baguette and salted butter he claimed came "from French virgins." And she said, "Do you mean it is secreted by French virgins, from their breasts and pores, or do you mean that nuns make it?"

"I'd like to think the former," he said and got up to put on an album of what he called French café music and pour boiling kettle water into his hand-press coffee maker. His coffee was always strong.

They avoided their mutual friends. They met at out-of-the-way places: late at night at the poolside bar of the funky motel on South Congress with its enormous winking candles and occasional bride and groom sashaying by still in costume, or in the afternoon at a café she knew off the old railroad tracks which served yerba mate around overturned wooden cable spools. They took long walks on unkempt dirt paths, mosquitoes buzzing at their ankles, but on the outskirts southeast of town, shunning the many city paths filled with zealous joggers and bikers, not only because they didn't want to be spotted but also because such contemporary urbanity didn't seem to jive with his sensibility, his fedoras and vintage suits. Even though she understood it to be vaguely ridiculous and pretentious in its way, Leda adored seeing him in his element, in places where he fit, timeless and right, like why museums have different rooms for different periods rather than mixing pieces all willy nilly.

They did things people in their situation did. They talked about what was in front of their faces or what was in the newspaper or what they thought about albums and books, Morrissey and Jorie Graham and the progress of his Land Art piece, and that was all they talked about. Leda was happy.

Russell's head would be resting on her belly and he would look at her askance and say, "Feelings light up like fireflies," but excitedly, as if this were a normal coupling, only waiting until the right time to come out to friends and family. Only once did he mention Adam, and she said quickly, "That isn't for you," although she didn't really mean it. It just felt like the appropriate thing, like the thing an engaged woman should say, the part she should be in control of. She didn't think it was becoming to admit indecision or fear of loss. She was ideologically opposed to falling apart. She was happy.

When Adam called, he no longer pushed Leda to set a date for the wedding or for her arrival in New York. He was biding his time, waiting for everything to blow over.

"How are the swans?" he asked.

"Still nesting, although I haven't been by to see them."

"That's not like you."

"I was going to go the other day, but something happened," she said. "This dog died right in front of me and then things just didn't feel right. It's hard to explain."

"Go see them soon and report back. I think about them all the time."

When she got off the phone, Leda heard the woman on her floor of the boarding house crying again, but the cardboard box of sick person things had been removed, shepherded into the dank, marijuana-scented depths of the woman's room, smaller and cheaper than Leda's own. The hallway smelled of flowers: bouquets of condolence. Leda did not ask.

Angélica had thrown her first Cinco de Mayo party in college—she filled piñatas with miniature bottles of tequila, somehow not realizing that when everyone hit the pastel-papered animals with an aluminum bat, the bottles would break and shatter, spraying the guests with liquor and slivers of glass. But she still threw Cinco de Mayo parties, although the events had become more staid, better planned.

Her party that year was the first time Russell and Leda appeared together in public since the night they'd met, although they arrived separately and made a concerted effort all evening to avoid even appearing like friends. Leda felt the special awareness of her hands that came with wearing new rings: heavy, silver, geometric pieces she'd bought the day before in one of those delusions where she convinced herself she deserved such things. For what? She would ask herself later. For being alive? For the same reasons I pretend to deserve Russell?

The apartment was strung with brightly colored paper banners, and bowls of guacamole were scattered on every available surface. Angélica wore a gauzy sequined blouse the design of which she described as "half Mexican, half 80s coke party" and Russell and Leda spent almost the entire time on opposite sides of the room getting plastered and trading coy, expressionless glances like unblinking china dolls. A contest of indifference. It was the most fun she'd had at a party, maybe ever.

"Do you see that guy in there?" he asked, when they finally ended up alone on the balcony smoking, drunk. "With the lamb chops?"

"Yes. The creationist," she said, stroking the back of his leg where no one could see. She was ready to leave the party. She was ready to follow him anywhere.

"Is he? Well, I caught him in the kitchen with his hand up the skirt of the woman wearing all the Squash Blossom turquoise."

"The woman who never learned how to whistle."

"Do you have a sound byte for everyone?" he asked.

"Not everyone," she told him. She pointed out the man who read books on reclaiming one's masculinity. The guy with the nose ring who owned no fewer than fifteen leather jackets. The woman whose refrigerator was filled entirely with fancy sauces: Mango Curry Sauce, Champagne Shallot Mustard, Vidalia Onion Fig Sauce.

"Don't such reductive characterizations strike you as unfair?" he asked, but playfully.

"Ah, so you're the man who believes people are complex. That's too bad because I am very, very simple," she said, biting her lips she wanted him so badly. "I'm the woman who's going to take a leak and then slip out of the party with a handsome arborist."

As she made her way inside, snippets from the crowd swam up around her: someone proclaiming the death of libraries; a woman talking about her post-divorce celebration trip to Guatemala with Angélica; "even most educated Americans assume Cinco de Mayo celebrates Mexican independence." The new rings felt tight and constricting as her fingers began to swell from so much drinking; margarita sugary-sweet lime taste coated her teeth.

Waiting in line for the bathroom, Leda squatted to look in the fish tank; blue and oily, the two companions propelled themselves in circles around the requisite pink castle. Why always pink, she wondered. Does that color have a calming influence on fish? Like the opposite of bulls and red? But suddenly one fish, the one with darker fins, began to float, to rise slowly to the top like an ascending scuba diver, and soon the second fish had followed suit until they were both flaccidly bobbing along the surface. A minute passed, and she could no longer deny the evidence. They were belly up. They were dead. The motherfucking fish were dead. As if her act of looking had done them in, as if her eyes emitted deadly lasers or her person was encased in a noxious cloud.

Leda quickly found the little mesh net on the shelf and fished them out of the freakishly blue tank and carried them through the party, drops of water scattering in her wake, out onto the balcony where, before any of the smokers could even open their mouths, she flicked the net and tossed the two of them in a perfect arc into the glossy, amorphous swimming pool down below.

Part of her understood the folly in this: how would a chlorinated, cement-enclosed pool have any chance of reviving them? But it was the closest she could get to the ocean and the feeling of releasing them back into the wild. She wanted that euphoria found in sappy movies when the dolphin is set free from the net or the Biblical ecstasy of a dove rising out of one's palm with the throbbing muscularity of slow-motion wing thrusts. Instead, she stood there gripping the rail, crying just enough to make her party-mascara run down her face. Someone eventually fetched Angélica who came and wrapped her arms around Leda's bony shoulders. And all she could think about was the swans perched on their nest, oblivious to the danger that surrounded them. She would not go see them again. They were better off without her.

Leda spent the first few days after the Cinco de Mayo party alone in her makeshift room listening to the answering machine. Adam said they needed to talk, that she just couldn't withdraw like this, she needed to act like an adult and work things through. Her boss said they needed to talk, that she was out of sick days, he knew she missed her fiancé and would put in a good word for her in New York. Russell said they needed to talk, that he didn't understand what happened, what he'd done wrong. Angélica said, "Bitch, call me."

Leda never considered someone a friend until he or she had criticized her to her face. That's how she knew who her friends were: they were comfortable enough to say: you look like hell; you're acting like a slut; you need to get your shit together. By the time someone could say these things without annoyance or exasperation, it was understood she loved Leda anyway. And then Leda could trust half of the good things she occasionally said too. Angélica, however, took this philosophy to the extreme; she considered herself a real no-bullshit kind of woman. She'd say, "Red lipstick makes you look like you're trying too hard," and so Leda would give her the gold tube she'd bought on sale at the mall—Angélica's skin was darker; she was Puerto Rican—and wonder if that was what her friend had wanted all along.

For the last several years, since the three of them moved to Austin—first Angélica to work for the local paper and then Adam and Leda for his graduate school—her fiancé and she existed on the periphery of Angélica's ever-larger people network; she was their confidante, separately, and the extent of their large-party entertainments, but otherwise, they ran in different social circles. Adam and Leda liked to drink considerably more and more often than Angélica did, and they had become increasingly cynical, disdainful even, of the wide-eyed hippies who still existed in that town with all their tender earnestness and food co-ops.

But twice a week Leda used to get off early from the library and sometimes dropped by Angélica's, at the old apartment, to drink coffee and gossip. Angélica's dining room table was always covered with a film of cigarette ash and china saucers overflowing with gaudy costume jewelry she tossed on and off her wrists and fingers throughout the day. She worked from home and usually returned from the gym around that time and sat drinking an enormous mug of Fair Trade dark roast, which she had to continue microwaving to combat the lower temperature caused by the milk she added to the coffee in stages, and smoking exactly four cigarettes.

"It's what allows me to be free," she liked to say, dramatically, as if it were her own piece of eastern wisdom, whenever Leda raised her eyebrows at the obsessive-compulsiveness of it all. "As long as I have my own place with its own order to come home to, then I can do anything everywhere else." And, it seemed she did. She traveled abroad for weeks on freelance gigs for rich people travel magazines and, if you believed her stories, moved in with men she met on the plane, camped out in the jungle in search of leopards, did drugs—"eight-dollar eight-balls"—for days at a time.

Leda knew, sitting in that kitchen on those afternoons staring at the Mondrian-like paintings, that Angélica had similar moments of intimacy with Adam—they went running together sometimes; they met for lunch; they had been friends first—but that didn't stop Leda from confessing things about him, about their relationship. "He thinks therapy is for the dim-witted and the dense. He thinks we're too self-actualized or something."

"A lot of good that's doing you."

"And these jobs he's applying for all over the country without consulting me—as if we didn't already move here for him," Leda would say, taking a cigarette from the pack on the table even though she'd quit, wondering if Angélica would tell him that too, that she was smoking again.

"He says you can get a librarian job almost anywhere whereas architecture doesn't work that way."

"Maybe I don't want to get a job just anywhere."

"I see what you're saying, Leda," Angélica would tell her. "Who does he think he is to be the one in control, right?"

Leda admitted there might be another reason. She knew Adam loved her—which was not to say he couldn't be prickly and biting when hurt—but sometimes she couldn't help wonder if he was marrying her because he needed someone and she was just who'd happened to come along. Like a dog, loyal to his owner merely because that was who picked him up from the pound. Maybe she was pressing the geography issue to prove he was not merely falling in with her but choosing her.

"Or maybe prove to yourself that you're choosing him?"

Angélica was a strange person to discuss these things with—she had sex with men, and she had intensely intimate relationships with men, but not the same men. She felt the two shouldn't be mixed, that sex caused a relationship to become possessive and critical and secretive. She wanted to be the person who knew everything. Occasionally Leda had agreed with her, decided Angélica was more philosophically evolved than most people. But then Leda would think: doesn't she realize when she says she wants everything, what she's most likely to have at the end of the day is nothing.

But even so, ever since Leda became engaged, she'd suspected Angélica pitied her in some way. Maybe that was the reason, sitting in the kitchen of her friend's newer, redder apartment after the Cinco de Mayo party was over and after she'd calmed down from her crying jag over the fish, she'd told Angélica about Russell. Maybe Leda thought romantic deception would impress her. But all Angélica said was, "I suppose it's no surprise. You always have been dependent on men." And so later, listening to her messages, curled up on her boarding house bed, Leda knew she'd have to face Adam and her boss and even Russell, but not Angélica. There was a point at which criticism no longer made someone a friend. Lying there staring at the ceiling, Leda felt racked by anger toward everyone.

After a few days Leda showed up at Russell's house. She lay down on his porch swing. She took a nap until he pulled into the driveway and picked her up in his arms, carrying her over his shoulder like a sack of potatoes. They sat in his kitchen and made a huge salad: artichoke, sun-dried tomatoes, arugula, avocado and chunks of pecan and goat cheese. They drank beer and washed the dishes searching for birds out the window and then sat on the floor flipping through old records. They pretended things were the same. They pretended they were a They.

She asked him about his Land Art piece, and he said he was finished, practically finished, a few more touches and it would be ready for the exhibition two weeks from then. She asked him about what he'd told her the night they'd met, at the housewarming party, about trying to explore the communication between humans and the natural world.

"I remember you said something about how they tame each other. Who do you think is more powerful really—us or them?"

"It's not about power, Leda. It's about us all being part of living world, a constellation of connection," he said.

"That is the cheesiest thing I've ever heard."

"Well, it's like those swans of yours nesting in a man-made park."

"Now you're just trying to get me in bed."

Russell had worked a double and so he fell asleep early, soundly, the sleep of the dead. Leda walked around the house wishing there were a television to watch or a magazine to read, but there were only heavy books staring from their hoods like brooding sentinels, and so eventually, she slipped off her clothes and lay next to him. She dozed in and out.

At some point during the night, she was jarred awake by a dark movement out of the corner of her eye, a swooping shadow across the ceiling. A bird? No, a bat. She tried to shake Russell awake, but he wouldn't budge and so she stood up, which caused the bat to become even more erratic, throwing itself off the walls like a pinball machine from hell. With a broom she started going at it, broad lunging motions overhead, and he dodged and squeaked and darted into the hallway and then the kitchen. The window was open and she thought she'd unlatch the screen and shoo him out that way, but in the meantime he became more aggressive, flapping at her head which was fucking awful and so she just swung right at him, she backed him into the pantry and then—and she had no idea where this came from—she began to truly pummel the thing until it flapped helplessly on the floor and eventually was still.

When she slunk back into the bedroom, Russell was groggily sitting up, tightly wrapped in the Nepalese bedspread.

"What's going on in there? What time is it?"

"Nothing. Go back to sleep," she said, pulling on her jeans.

He narrated her half-hearted attempt to leave, playfully though, in that way of a man aware he has no claim. "Russell, there is an emergency at the library. You know, one of those big-time library emergencies, and I must go this instant," he said, mimicking her voice as he searched for pants of his own. "You're a super lady, Russell. Don't call me, I'll call you."

"There's no reason for you to get dressed," said Leda.

"I will not be outmatched for armor."

She succumbed. They lay back down in all their clothes and fell asleep, not touching but curled around each other like worms, and he murmured, "You didn't go," and for a moment she was happy again. In the morning, she stuffed the dead bat into a plastic bag and was out the door before he woke up.

The woman on Leda's floor moved out and the door to that room was left open so prospective residents could see inside, sunlight reflecting off dust particles in the air. Russell called and left messages on the answering machine, a litany of clichés: you can't have your cake and eat it too; you made your bed now lie in it; like a bull in a china shop. One at a time, night after night, he called and said one sentence like that, just one, and then hung up, until one day he stopped calling altogether, and she wasn't sure if he'd run out of truisms or if he'd finally given up on her for good. When a romance is over, she wondered, why do we use the phrase "to leave" someone? As if people were places from where we come and go.

Leda didn't step foot outside the boarding house for a week. Then, one day she decided to walk the three blocks to the neighborhood hole-in-the-wall for a beer. Baby steps, she told herself. Baby steps.

She didn't usually like going to bars alone because a woman by herself attracts unwanted attention; it was like continuously having to swat away flies. Especially Leda: pretty much anything looked good on her. She decided that particular trip would be a lesson in how to make her expression hard, how to look so standoffish and unapproachable no one would even feel comfortable sitting on the barstool next to her. The place was rustic and dim and mostly empty. She sat up against the wall, her chest scooped in on itself. She thought of her mother, a teetotaler who had gone with Leda's father to bars so as to keep an eye on him, always perched in rigid disapproval.

"We called it off," she overheard one man tell another. The two seemed to have run into each other at random, to be talking about a wedding. "She has a kid, you know, and I just wasn't ready for the responsibility."

"Heavy" said the other one, who was wearing a "Keep Austin Weird" t-shirt.

"You know how it is," the man said. "I want to start clean."

Leda ordered another Negra Modelo. The bartender, who had picked up on her eavesdropping, whispered into her ear as if by way of some explanation, "Venus is in retrograde." She nodded. She smoked cigarette after cigarette, lighting another before the first one was finished. Starting clean? Who in the hell ever starts clean?

It was several hours before the Land Art exhibition was scheduled to begin when Leda pulled up to the gate of the cemetery. She had never seen Russell's piece, but he had described it to her: "undulating piles of seeds and pecans crisscrossed by rivulets of polished stones." She found it after a few minutes; the piece was organic, everything rounded and even as it swirled through the patchwork of grave markers. It was almost too perfect. But it had been made by a human hand, which in a way meant it was as natural as anything else, she supposed. Was it even possible for something that existed at all to be unnatural? Wasn't everything in the world somehow an expression of the mechanisms of life being lived?

It was sweltering hot, and she found a spot some yards away beneath a dogwood, sweat collecting behind her knees; bark scraped her back as she struggled to get comfortable;

ants scuttled down her shorts. She waited. She pretended she didn't know what she was waiting for but, eventually, hours later, as people began to crowd the path through the cemetery, he finally showed up. He was wearing white linen and a straw hat, dressed as if on safari before the Second World War, and he was with Angélica. They were holding hands, but not holding exactly, rather their palms lightly skimmed each other's, fingers wiggling and dancing, but slowly, rhythmically, like tiny hypnotized serpents. Leda thought to herself: a person is not sympathetic or unsympathetic because of how he or she treats you—we are good to each other for bad reasons and horrible to each other for good ones. That was what she told herself.

"It won't be long now," she said over the phone. "Hours."

"Look for the man with his arm full of lilies," he replied.

The newspaper in her lap had a headline reading "Welcome!!!," and a half-page color photograph of the cygnets with their lead-colored beaks, downy and bizarre, bunched tightly around the puffed breasts of their parents. There were six of them, originally seven but the runt hadn't made it. Leda didn't feel responsible. She hadn't been to see them once since Adam left over three months ago.

As she looked around her room—the furniture that came with the place stripped of her few, meager possessions— and as she fanned herself with the thick paper of the plane ticket, she knew what would happen when she got to New York. She was not entirely ready to face it, but she knew. She was going there, but it didn't matter. Staying and going were really the same thing for her. She folded the photograph of the swans and put it in the back pocket of the only jeans she had left that still fit comfortably, rubbing her small, new belly with the other hand, and thought to herself: Life will always be this way. Even when it isn't.

LYING IN A HAMMOCK, FIRST DAY OF SPRING, APPRECIATING ISSA

BY MARTIN ARNOLD

Another season of vines clinging
to wind-sheared limbs the breeze swings,

another season of fledgling posturing and preening

and I couldn't choose a better station
to surf the channels of this breeze

a few feet above turf
where spring grass is greenest.

Above me, thousand-mile-long misunderstandings.

Back among the trees, a rusted rim
bent under its last sweet dunk.

And I can't help but feast on my good luck

as another season's mosquitoes
cloud the air above my mouth

before I pass right through their bodies.

CIRCLES INSIDE LARGER CIRCLES

BY MARTIN ARNOLD

Monks moving mowers that forge
thousands of linked rings one blade wide,

monks perched in oak branches rustling their wings,
monks splitting a mountain

of firewood into larger mountains, monks passing through
    solid wood
doorways. With robes tucked into their waists

like petals peeled back on pale stamens,
monks guide rivers inside flexing green tunnels.

Harvest moons rising beyond rolling hills of cabbage
or azaleas sheltered beneath one hundred waxy umbrellas

cupping yesterday's showers, each monk's an individual flame
the breeze could extinguish though collectively they set the
    neighborhood

ablaze. Through a wall of interlocking steel diamonds
tufts of grass cut a middle path down the gravel

in the driveway. Monks shuck golden coffers, polish worm-
    eaten hearts
that bulge like clouds in the sails of their robes.

Monks brush scarab beetles jewelling the ferns
into their palms. It must take a lifetime

to love this world
this much.

PEOPLE OF THE LIBRARY

BY MARTIN ARNOLD

Should float away beneath ballooning craniums,
Should carry heavy tomes to tether them.
Instead, this one cartwheels down the aisle
Thump thump thumping like a flat tire.
That one parts a dictionary to helmet it.
That one applies two-volume deodorant sticks.
Book pillows, chin rests, drool catchers.
Booster chairs, staircases, desk separators.
Books at hips like holstered guns.
And this one through her bound window steps
To feel the stories rush by
As bigger and bigger the end gets.

WE'RE ALL SEARCHING FOR SOMETHING

BY MARTIN ARNOLD

Past the man with ponytail and eye patch
Beeping wide arcs in the sand,
Sounding the depths of its pockets;

Past the whisping legs of ladies briskly walking
Who believe Death doesn't own
A single pair of jogging shoes;

Past couples melting into waves of molten sunshine;

A woman raises her arms to fly
Fifteen competing gull kites
At the tips of bread fingers.

Past the boy emptying trash barrels
Near towels littered with bikinied girls;

Past the family with lines bobbing in the surf
That occasionally land them on the local diner's wall;

A man collects hooves of sea horses—
Coral, opaque, obsidian, bronze—

Horses that drive waves in their wake toward the beach.

Close your eyes, he says, you can feel
Strands of their wild manes stream by.

EVERYTHING MUST GO

BY RACHEL NEWCOMB

It's still dark outside when the alarm goes off, Mickey Mouse's white-gloved arms pointing to six. I slap at the dingy brass bells, no longer as pristine as they used to be when the clock adorned the nightstand in my cousin Carolyn's meringue-white bedroom. By the much tamer standards of the seventies, Carolyn was spoiled, with her matching white wicker furniture and a Barbie dream palace, luxuries afforded her because her father wore ties and worked in a firm. His brother, my own father, owned only one tie: wide, burgundy, and dotted with golf clubs, suitable for neither weddings nor funerals, which did not stop him from wearing it to both. There was some relationship, I gathered, between owning many ties and being able to afford a matching bedroom set for your daughter, rather than the foldout sofa I shared with my little brother.

Chester stirs, arching his back and pretending to be asleep. Gone are the days he was up all night, waking me on his prowls in search of a phantom mouse scratching a path behind the walls of the apartment. I push him away from my head, rolling out of the warm bed with the Ralph Lauren down comforter. The comforter: $10, a two-story Victorian, young couple, no children. Moving to a better place, or else on their way to a congenial divorce, I couldn't tell, and they resisted my gentle attempts to pry.

I run a comb through my hair and brush my teeth quickly, throwing on some sweatpants and a light sweater over my t-shirt. Florida winter mornings can be deceptively chilly, although by noon the sun makes everyone glad to have left behind the cold places where they used to live. At the kitchen table, I drink coffee and review the classified ads that I've circled the night before, along with directions printed out from the Internet. With a highlighter I draw a line to mark my path among the neighborhoods, cutting a swath among suburbs, apartment complexes, and neighborhoods that I know will be filled with McMansions.

Affluent neighborhoods usually have the best sales, but I don't discriminate.

The first ad takes me through a neighborhood of stucco villas with faux-cracked walls, perched on docks facing a glittering lake, one of the thousands you see from the air whose access is all but closed off to the public. Today an Eames chair is up for sale on Via Tuscany (I have this on inside information), and as I pull up to the address I see a bungalow slightly more modest than the villas surrounding it, one of the few surviving homes not swept away by a developer whose most prominent influence appears to be the Olive Garden.

It's five minutes to seven, the sun just beginning to touch the dewy golf-course lawns, but the driveway is crawling with garage sale enthusiasts, despite the ad's warning against early birds. Immediately I spot Dale and Marty climbing down from their SUV. Even this early, Dale wears all her makeup, her tiny frame draped in the latest casual weekend fashions. She's got the look of a woman with a lot of time and money on her hands, but she works hard for it, going to the gym at five every morning before she starts her job at a real estate agency, having her hair professionally frosted at the salon. Marty is all softness to her hard edges: middle-aged, balding, indistinct. Some smart real-estate decisions back in the 1980s put them in a neighborhood close to this one, a neighborhood of modest ranch houses whose value has shot up with the latest bubble. But they're aspirational, only attending sales in the best neighborhoods, curious about what people richer than they are consume. Not like me, content to live on the outskirts of town in an apartment complex, in a place just big enough to house my treasures, with an extra room for guests, should anyone ever decide to visit.

"Hello, Teresa," Dale greets me. "We're just discussing whether the estate sale over in College Park might have anything good."

"Overpriced Ethan Allen," I say. "I heard this from Patty." Patty makes it her business to call the estate sale companies each week. Sometimes she phones me if she hears about a sale I might like. I'm more mid-century modern myself, anything I can get my hands on that reminds me of that era with all its surface perfection. Mothers dressed in pearls and starched skirts dancing a *pas-de-deux* with their vacuums, the wonders of plastics, tables with antenna-like appendages suggesting the endless possibilities of the space age. By the time I was growing up, this world had disappeared, and brown shag carpets, waterbeds, and lava lamps settled in.

"I think we might check it out, Marty?" Dale proposes. Marty grunts. It's clear who wears the pants here, in this case a tight pair of jeans from Old Navy that Dale might have borrowed from her daughter. I've never understood what Marty does for a living. Dale claims he's in a managerial role with the Orlando Magic, but his mousiness leads me to picture him at practices hovering near the players, ready with a towel to wipe away their sweat, keeping the cooler always full of Gatorade.

"There's nothing special here," Dale assures me, gesturing back at the house. "Just a lot of baby stuff." I don't want to ask about the chair, don't want her to ruin what I know is probably true, that the chair has sold already, especially if this many early birds have already gotten their hands on the goods.

"One man's trash…" I say, and she offers a brittle smile. The phrase is a mantra we repeat, an acknowledgment of a shared tribal allegiance. We even have an Internet message board, with 796 local members at last count. I stick mostly to garage sales, avoiding the estates, where I know I'm rifling through the relics from dead people's lives. At those it's the curios that kill me, wooden Tiki-bar salt-and-pepper shakers, commemorative plates of crumbling Grecian ruins, canasta tables and crystal decanters. Souvenirs without anyone to remember them. I don't like picturing the fifty-year marriages, the grandchildren who only stopped by on trips to Disney, the migration from New York to Florida, from a rest home to the grave.

This bungalow has been emptied out and is even smaller inside than it appears from the front. In the back yard my eyes scan the items for sale: a baby crib, a few lamps, an ancient stereo, yard tools, and some toys. People are milling around, their hands mostly empty, not a good sign this early in the morning, when the best things should be here for the taking.

I don't see the Eames chair anywhere. I walk over toward the sales table, where a woman in her forties sits with a lock box in front of her. From across the yard another woman addresses her.

"Valerie, how much did we want for the George Foreman?"

"Five dollars," Valerie shouts back.

They could be friends, I surmise, but the "we" in the woman's question makes me think otherwise.

"I heard you had an Eames chair for sale," I say.

"Did it say that in the ad?" Valerie sounds surprised. "My partner was thinking of selling it, but she decided to have the movers take it over to the new house instead."

I absorb this information: no chair, a new house, a couple moving up and not out. I'm disappointed that in the gamble of choosing the first sale of the day, I've picked a bad one.

"How much for the red wagon?" I ask.

"It should be tagged." She gets up from the table and moves around to check on the wagon. "Twenty dollars."

It seems pricey. A high price usually means the person doesn't want to part with it.

"Your kids too big for it?" I say, trying to seem casual.

"See any kids around here?" she snaps. I lower my eyes. This will be the moment she scolds herself for reading too much into my question, I think. And I'm right.

"I'm sorry," she says. "You're right, they're too big for a wagon. And they live with their father now."

I love the details, when the conversations over objects lead to other places. The picture I have of them comes into sharper focus. I wonder if the marriage ended when Valerie realized she liked women, or if there was something else. But I'm not here to judge. In the mountains of junk Americans love to buy and hoard, the stories lie in what they're willing to part with.

I pick up a pair of yellow Mary Janes with a single daisy painted on each toe.

"My daughter's almost four," I lie. "I wonder if these would fit her."

"That's how old Kayla was when she wore them," Valerie says, her face lighting up. "We have some children's clothes over there." I move over to the rack, feigning interest in the clothes. The lie is only a partial one. Dora is almost twenty. I planned to be a better mother, but life just got in the way. Her father took off for the West Coast with rock star aspirations, and when it was time to sue for child support, he was nowhere to be found. For a while I left her with my mother, trying to stay in school (I studied architecture), but then dropping out of Rutgers when I realized I could make more money in the city without a degree.

My job as an executive assistant on Wall Street should have been enough to set us both up, especially back then, when New York didn't cost as much as it does now. But being tied down with a baby wasn't good for the direction I saw myself heading at the time, and the people I was running with outside working hours didn't want to hear about her. There was a point in the eighties when time seemed to speed up, when the economy was so strong that everyone could have a piece of the good times. I believed in that trickle-down effect Reagan used to talk about, because my Christmas bonuses showed it. At the firm I was indispensable, the one who could be counted on to run across town in stilettos to deliver a document or make sure that after work, there was always enough coke to go around.

When the downturn came I moved uptown, disconnecting myself from all the people I used to know. Suddenly it seemed everyone had families they went home to after work. I was finally ready for Dora, but it was too late. My mother had found a family from the church who couldn't have children of their own. I must have been in a fog when I signed those papers, but I couldn't get her back, and she didn't want to go. Dora had a pink canopy bed in her own room, and who could blame her? Everyone, including my mother, thought it was best if she didn't see me until she was older. It sent her mixed messages.

"Nobody blames you for giving her up," my mother said. "If that'd been an option when I was younger, I would have done the same thing, tried to give a better future to you kids." Instead, her shotgun marriage to my father was the example she set for me.

I went to see Dora one last time before I moved down here. When she came out of her classroom I spotted her immediately, a skinny little twig of a girl, her hair straight and dark like her father's. I called out to her and she separated from her friends, looking at me with her big gray eyes. Those eyes were mine; they were my best feature.

"You sure you don't want to move down to Florida with your mom?" I asked. "We can go to Disney every weekend."

"I like it here," she said, her expression flat, neutral. That was when she told me about the pink canopy bed, the computer, and the handmade dollhouse Mr. Bettinger had built for all the dolls they bought her. I thought about my cousin's Barbie dreamhouse, and one of the hand-me-downs that Carolyn gave me when we were kids, her cornsilk hair chopped off, a dog's teeth marks visible on her plastic belly. Like me, Carolyn had moved to the city, but she'd become a success, a lawyer with an apartment on Park Avenue, a husband, a son, and a nanny.

I wander away from the baby clothes and cast a final look around. There's nothing I want here. The two women seem happy, even without the kids. I imagine Valerie still gets to see them.

The second sale is in Winter Park Pines, a neighborhood filled with ranch houses built during my favorite era. I like the settled feel of the neighborhood, the spreading live oaks, and the houses that seem to sink back into their foundations. Yards filled with flowers year-round, scarlet bougainvillea tumbling over the walls, perfect green lawns. Ten years ago I could have bought something in the Pines, but I missed my chance, as the prices have skyrocketed. The road curves around, leading to a series of duplexes, and

I recognize this street from a retirement party I attended a few years ago for a colleague. I work in a busy doctor's office now, all obstetricians and gynecologists. It's a nice job, seeing the women who come in, faces and bellies both swollen with hope. Much better than working with doctors who treat cancer or heart disease.

My mother and I have an unspoken agreement that we don't talk about Dora, although she has agreed that if Dora comes looking, she'll tell her where I am. With the Internet I've been able to find out a few things about her. She's in college now, at Syracuse, and she's on the field hockey team. I never played a sport in my life, and neither did her father, though for all I know he could be a marathon-running record executive in L.A. by now. His name is too common to turn up much on the Internet, though, and any searches bounce back a million hits from Google.

This sale starts at eight, which officially makes me an early bird. It's ten minutes before the hour, and people are waiting outside. I look around for somebody I know and spot Patty pacing back and forth in front of the garage. She's about ten years older than I am, and she lives alone, with a couple cats, estranged from her family. Kids in other states who don't write or call. I try not to demonstrate my enthusiasm for garage sales as openly as Patty does, but still I'm here each week. I am a fan of design, and I was majoring in architecture before I dropped out of college, so there is some kind of trajectory in my interests today, even if I never made a career out of it.

"How's Chester?" she asks. She assumes my cat is the main man in my life.

"A little creaky," I say. "His years are showing."

"Miles was at the vet this week," she says. "His arthritis is bothering him, but the vet can't do much about that."

"Do you know anything about this sale?"

"Just what the ad said. Moving sale, everything must go."

The front door to the house opens. I try not to look too eager as I join the crowd funneling through the door. We pass through a narrow hallway that opens up into a room with a high ceiling and lots of skylights. The walls are white, the plush carpets the color of pale sand, and everything is immaculate.

I move to a corner of the room to get a better look. People are already grabbing at things without even looking. There are a few paintings, abstract with pale flowers and muted colors that do not clash with the overall décor. A price tag dangling off of one painting reads $300, meaning it's not something the owners really want to part with. A Mies Van Der Rohe chair starts my heart beating, its v-shaped steel frame cradling black leather cushions. The tag on this one reads $500, and I start to get annoyed; someone misrepresented the sale. These are estate sale prices.

People gather around the objects spread out on the dining table: Christmas ornaments, napkin rings, hand towels, knife sets. A set of lamps is the first to speak to me. Each lamp is a thin column of steel shooting up into white cylindrical shades, and they're overpriced but in perfect condition. I imagine them on either side of my bed, where I've recently acquired two Nelson end tables, circa 1954, with tapered aluminum bases and round, black tops. I grab both of the lamps, laying my claim. At a card table in the corner, a woman waits for the first customers, the cash box open in front of her.

"Can I put these here?" I ask. She nods and starts to say something, but I'm off again, my eye falling on a black espresso machine in the kitchen that nobody seems to have noticed. It's seventy dollars, enough to give most people pause, but I know better: it's a Gaggia, and like everything else, it appears to be in perfect condition. I lift it up and notice the set of *demitasse* cups beside it, also black, each tiny cup with a thin silver ring around the top.

"Can I help you with those?" The woman has moved out from behind the card table and is at my side. She's in her fifties at least, and still beautiful, with delicate blue eyes and sharp features, her silver-blonde hair the color of Barbie's. I wonder if it's her house: a divorce, perhaps? She's too young to be moving into a retirement community.

There are no men present, except the reluctant ones who've been dragged here by their wives. Perhaps her husband has left her for somebody younger.

"Thank you," I say, handing her the cups.

"I just don't want them to break. These are my sister's things," she volunteers. "I'll throw in the cups for ten dollars more if you buy the coffee maker."

"Deal," I say. "And your sister is…" I look around for someone else who seems to belong here.

"Dead," she finishes.

"I'm sorry. I didn't know this was an estate sale."

"It isn't," she tells me, "An estate sale seemed too final somehow."

"But these are very nice things," I say. "Most people coming to garage sales are looking for a bargain."

"We're hoping her possessions will go home with the right people," she tells me, looking me over. "People who will appreciate and cherish them. Not those who are trying to profit from our misfortune. That's why we didn't do an estate sale."

"Oh," I say. But still I feel misled.

"Sallie had cancer. Within six months she was gone. She was never sick as a child. I was the one people would have expected to come down with something like that. Everything that came around, I got." The woman tells me about her childhood ailments, the high-risk pregnancy, the cholesterol and blood pressure issues that her sister never had. Then she starts talking about her sister, the hospital, the chemo. How the day she died it was eighty-five degrees, even though it was November. It didn't seem like a day for dying, when the weather was so nice and everywhere people were swimming and going to Disney. I calculate: it's been two months. The coffee cups on the tray in her hand clatter slightly.

"Let me take those," I say.

"Eighty-five degrees," she tells me, as if we are old friends. "When we left the hospital, there were all these birds squawking overhead. I guess they were migrating somewhere. And it was so hot. Do you like coffee?"

I'm not expecting the suddenness of her question.

"As much as the next person," I say. "I like a good espresso."

"So did Sallie," the woman volunteers. "She lived in Italy for many years. She was an artist, you know. Did all those paintings you see on the wall."

"Oh," I say. "They're very nice."

"Would you like to take a closer look?" I feel a mix of discomfort and sympathy that I'm not used to feeling. This is not why I come to these sales. I come more for the sense of change, to see how things separate: objects from people, people from people. But still I like to think of the people being in the world, not dead, only separate from one another.

"They're a little beyond my budget," I say. "But very nice. You shouldn't sell them. You'll be glad later that you kept them."

"My house is full. I could never find room for them. But I like you. I think you should have one."

We stand in front of one of the paintings, and I try to let it speak to me, to tell me something about the woman who painted it, but all I see is a mix of delicate, long-stemmed flowers done in watercolor against a beige background.

"I'll give it to you," she says. "I'll take your name and number, and then if I want to see it later, I can call you."

"Really, I don't think I'm the one," I say. "I don't know where I'd put it, either. I've got too much." She looks surprised that I would refuse her gift, although if gifts are obligations, this is one I'm not sure I want to take on. With the other objects there is the sense of keeping something in use, the lightbulbs in the lamps still the ones she used before me, the espresso machine spilling out cup after cup of hot coffee, keeping me awake and alive.

Later, when I'm at home, I notice a blank space on the wall in the guest room where the picture would have fit perfectly. The white space taunts me when I go in to clean, so for a while I shut the door and avoid the room entirely. The guest room waits for someone on the cusp of adulthood to inhabit it, in case Dora decides to stop by, in case she calls me up on her way to a Florida spring break with her friends. I keep some young-adult novels in the bookshelf, next to a well-worn Snoopy. Her tastes will be different from mine, girlish and not modern, so there's a flowered Laura Ashley comforter on the bed, an antique Edwardian dressing table with an oval mirror where I can picture her brushing her long, chestnut-colored hair. Thanks to garage sales, the room keeps pace with the stages of Dora's life, with what she might be interested in. Each year I redecorate, storing away childish things for the day when I finally hold a sale of my own, when I'll tell people the truth: my daughter's almost grown up, she's away from home and doesn't need these things anymore.

NEAR YUCCA FLATS

BY JOHN NIZALOWSKI

Walking through
dying Joshua trees,
decaying branches
like severed limbs,
I find a half-burned
Penthouse in an
abandoned camp.

Hiroshima,
Salem,
Joan of Arc.

Above me,
water has carved
yonic caves in
the gray shale
canyon walls.
Grass grows
green there,
the creosote bush
banished to the
scrublands.

Fifty years ago,
atomic fire seared
the dark horizon,
now red in the
mountain sunset.

Across the canyon,
a jack donkey defends
his two wild jennies.
They stand as a holy
trinity while the sacred
night descends,

his warning cough
loudly echoes.

This is what we should
all do, instead of
burning our mothers.

The Poet's Apprentice

By John Nizalowski

(for Isadora Nizalowski)

A landscape of sharp
shadows, rocks, a silent
volcano. Rattle of golden
chains, geese circling home,
a silver spire crumbling
at the base, the clash of
armies, sigh of nightfall,
the cinnamon dust of
Egypt seeking its master.

On the red desert,
the little Buddha soul,
my daughter,
smiling with the wisdom
the rest of us have
forgotten, flings sand
into the air, knows
well the void from
which she's arrived,
and so bears a message.

Dorado

By Tatjana Soli

We won the fishing trip in a drinking contest. The way it was supposed to work, after you drank six margaritas in a row, the bartender dropped your name in a fish bowl, and at the end of the night, the cocktail waitress, Marcy, drew out a winner. But we had been playing for the last thirteen nights, losing each time—Kent heroically shit-faced each night—and the bartender took pity and cheated, throwing the chits of paper with the other drunks' names in the trash bin, under the discarded olive pits, orange rinds, mint leaves, and maraschino cherries of his trade. A real philosopher, he said that anyone so misguided to try so hard for so little, over and over, deserved a break.

We accepted the trip with no compunction and zero moral hand-wringing. Why should some other sad sack enjoy sitting out in the fight chair, sipping beer in the hot sun, when we'd depleted our traveler's checks to pay the exorbitant bar bill since we arrived nearly two weeks ago? We had visions of a record-breaking marlin hanging upside down on the dock, flashbulbs going off, cell phones and digital cameras preserving the event for posterity, and then a storage freezer of fillets, each bundled in its own white paper shroud. Enough meat to last us until.... to last us.

"My Superman," I would say. "My Clark Kent." Our little joke. Instead of water into wine, he would turn tequila into fish.

When we first arrived in Mexico, stoic, we had tried to experience the country, had left the resort and gone into town, but everywhere we went we saw flocks of begging, black-haired children, and the ones who didn't beg off us sold pieces of paper and balloons for absurdly small amounts, and this was even worse than the begging, and pretty soon we just ended up eating in the hotel restaurant. When we weren't in the bar. We had been married fourteen years, but the manager insisted on upgrading us to the honeymoon suite despite our protests. Balefully we stared at each other across the huge, heart-shaped mattress. Although we still loved each other, we slept on opposite sides, our backs to each other. A phase. This ill-gotten fishing junket seemed like a vacation from our vacation, a way out of the barren impasse we had reached in our life.

A threadbare year ago, I had been carpooling our two children to field hockey and play rehearsals. We were backed-up on the freeway exit ramp when a semi lost control and plowed into a car three cars back. A ripple of destruction and pain, instant death so there wasn't even a good-bye, and the thing that I can forgive least is the fact that I survived. I told Kent that I was sorry every morning, until the therapist insisted that I stop.

Captain Bob phoned our room at five a.m., and my heart froze, thinking some new disaster had befallen us, until I remembered that couldn't be, that we were on vacation, a time when the universe supposedly bends the rules. People don't get cancer or die on vacation. At least not that you hear about.

"Be at the boat at six. We're heading to a sandbar for a little shark," he said, and hung up before I could ask how little said shark would be. I begged off the trip to Kent's receding back as he headed for the shower.

"You promised to try things," he said. "Maybe this will be Life-Altering."

I didn't want Life-Altering, but I got out of bed anyway. I had to do my Lois Lane best. At six a.m. we walked up and down the wormy dock, looking for the *Knot Done*, repeatedly passing a broken-down-looking sportfisher, until finally a man yelled up from the galley, "You're here!"

Now, I know nothing about boats except what I've seen on television, *Miami Vice* reruns in particular, so boat was synonymous in my mind with drug yacht, which this wasn't. Too small for one, and top-heavy, like it would tip over in a big wave. Wasn't a big wave always in the offing? No gleaming wood, only yellowing fiberglass, and even that had seen better days—with darker brown stains caused by unmentionable, unthinkable events.

The only way to get from the nose of the boat to the back was heel-toeing along a narrow ledge against the galley, with only a stainless-steel railing that came to your knees as if to trip you on purpose. One grabbed handholds to keep from being pitched overboard and held on for dear life. No problem while sitting in the dock, big problem when the boat was banging along full speed, the ledge slick with spray.

But once I clambered to the back, I realized there was little reason to go there. The floor was rippled like a washboard, large gutters ran down the sides, and there was a large slab, like an operating table, and that's what it was—a place to slice-and-dice the catch, drain out the blood, scoop away the entrails, chop off the head—dumping it all into the ocean. A portable stockyard. Yuck.

"So what's this about shark?" Kent said affably, opening an offered beer, at six-fifteen in the morning. Only I knew the closest that my Clark Kent had gotten to a fish was opening a can of tuna, but I said nothing.

Like his boat, Captain Bob had also seen better days. "Oh, nothing. The *charter* wants to try for one, but it's beyond him. We'll go out to the sandbar and watch dolphins, nothing more."

"Too bad," Kent said. "I was kinda hoping for a marlin."

"Only if the paying part of the excursion gets his first." Captain Bob waved as a young Mexican man, small and wiry, his skin the color of burnt toast from sun exposure, jumped on the boat. "Sally. This is Sally."

The young man looked down at his feet as he shook hands with us. "Salvador," he said.

"In this country, we use American names," Bob said. Never mind that we happened to be in Mexico, or that the chosen name was a woman's. Sally had bowed legs, walking awkwardly on land, but once on the boat, he moved like a sleek seal through water.

"Where you folks from?" Captain Bob asked, not waiting for the answer.

"San Diego," I said, stalling to figure out how to get back to my room and under the sheltering covers of my bed.

Bob stopped and turned around with more energy than I'd seen in him so far. "Lived in San Berdoo myself. You couldn't *give* me California. Couldn't get me to go back."

We said nothing. I didn't guess too many people were exactly begging for Captain Bob's return. Just as I was trying to think of an excuse to ditch the whole trip, the *charter*, his wife, and three kids banged on the side of the boat.

"Ahoy, there," the man said.

Because, of course, the resort wasn't going to give us a free, daylong boat excursion: the cost of the diesel alone ruled that out. No, we were being attached to the family bucking up for the whole trip—Dick and Trisha Hornberg, with their kids, Frankie Senior, Frankie Junior, and Betsy.

One beer down, Captain Bob was looking rougher by the minute, and a kind of reek was coming off his crusted clothes as the sun heated the air around us. I thought of one of those crustacean things on the wildlife shows that look so fierce and warrior-like underwater, so improbable and helpless when taken out of it.

"Fishing passengers are one thing," Bob said, stifling a burp. "But no kids."

"I paid for the kids," Dick said.

Captain Bob drew off his cap and combed back his thinning, greasy hair into a ponytail. "Read the contract. The hotel clearly inhibits liability for minors."

"This is a family outing."

Captain Bob took his elbow and moved him a step aside, but spoke even louder and more clearly for us all to overhear. "This is a warrior's pursuit. Man against violent nature. Danger and death. Facing the void. Are you prepared to expose your kids to all that, Dick?"

"That's fine," he said. "I'll accept that."

"Please put it in writing," Bob said, suddenly a cool and distant customer, morphing from pirate philosopher into one of Melville's bureaucrats.

"And here's for your trouble," Dick said, stuffing a hundred-dollar bill into Captain Bob's sagging shirt pocket. One had to admire how if Captain Bob even noticed, he gave no sign of it.

Dick wrote out a few sentences on the back of a brochure for sunset cruises and handed it over.

"This, sir, will count as a pudendum to the original, officiating contract." With that, Captain Bob climbed the ladder to the flybridge, sheltering under the bimini top while the rest of us stood stunned in the baking sun. An empty bottle flew overhead into the sea.

Okay, this isn't the nicest way to describe them, but the Hornbergs reminded me of the Pillsbury Dough Family—all white and puffy, small eyes buried in fat cheeks. The husband had a potbelly, the wife had pillowy breasts and hips, and the kids had dimpled elbows and hands, thick little legs that made them waddle rather than walk straight. The girl was thirteen, with pimpling skin and a bulky training bra under her T-shirt that she tugged, like a horse getting used to a bridle. The boys were younger, ten and eight, and I never did find out who the original Frankie namesake was.

Once we left the dock, we all retreated in different directions of our little tub/prison. Kent climbed the ladder to join Captain Bob, Dick sat in the fighting chair and glared out at the adversarial ocean, the two boys plopped down into puddles of flesh on the deck, and played on their electronic gameboards. Betsy sprawled out on the sofa-ette in the galley, puzzling over a teen magazine.

After ten minutes of standing in the sun, admiring the water and the receding shoreline, sniffing in the diesel fumes, Trisha and I both crawled into the shade of the galley.

"Glad to have someone around for some girl talk," Trisha said, and I smiled thinly.

Trisha proceeded to unpack her grocery sack of chips, cookies, candy bars, cracker-cheese combos. She must have bought out a convenience store of all its junk food. I realized that Kent and I hadn't given a thought to food; in fact, if we wanted to eat we'd have to depend on the largesse of the Hornbergs.

"What brings you to Mexico?" Trisha asked, as she doled out bags to each of her recumbent children, as if she worried that a hiatus in their feeding would starve them.

"It was the cheapest thing available. Off season. And the liquor is cheap."

The therapist had insisted I be more forthcoming about my feelings so now I had a kind of Tourette's of the truth. Trisha laughed, a real bray that conveyed either stupidity, or that she worried about her own and her brood's safety around people who answered questions in a way that so deviated from social niceties.

"That's funny. Isn't this the best place? We've had such a great time."

"Yeah." I didn't think this was remotely the best place.

"So really—what brings you two lovebirds down here?" she asked.

"I guess it's an anniversary, of sorts," I said, still stunned by the lovebird comment, because that's one thing I didn't think anyone would mistake our being. Anymore. Even though in high-school we were voted most romantic couple and until last year all our friends said we had the happiest marriage they knew.

Trisha clapped her hands, her big diamond wedding ring flashing in the light, and I squinted in its glare.

"I knew it! Besides, you two got the Honeymoon Suite. Stole it right out from under Dick and me."

I looked away, embarrassed for both of us, and watched as Betsy dug in her bag of Cheetos, eating them one at a time. Unfortunately, she rubbed her face as she read, leaving a fluorescent haze of orange behind like a bad self-tanning cream. Trisha followed my gaze and then pounced on her daughter.

"Filthy, filthy," she said, brushing at Betsy's face and hands, dragging her onto her feet. "Wash you face and go play with your brothers."

"Kids," Trisha said, and shrugged, and I shrugged back.

If I were Betsy's mother, I would have ripped the bag of Cheetos out of the girl's hand and dumped the whole toxic picnic into the ocean. How about some green salad, how about some sunblock, for Christ's sake, to protect that pale, wobbly skin the texture of boiled peanuts?

"You're so lucky to not have kids yet," Trisha said, winking, and suddenly the pounding of the boat caught my stomach, the hangover and the sleepiness too much, and I felt fragile and brittle inside.

"I don't feel so well."

"What's wrong? Do you need something to eat? How about a boiled egg?"

I'll give her this, she even peeled the shell off and sprinkled the top with salt before she handed it to me.

"Thank you," I said, but my stomach, like a changeling, was already on to something else, and the egg in my hand was so revolting I couldn't look at it.

"Enjoy this time alone," Trisha said. She leaned over, leering at me. "I could use some romancing, let me tell you."

I am the victim of an over-active imagination, hence the prescriptions for sedatives, sleep-aids, and anti-depressants, none of which I took, and I saw that, yes, Trisha's big-breasted, wide-hipped, long–legged body, all the way down to her wide feet with toenails lacquered orange-red, all suggested a voraciousness and lust that Dick was unlikely to be equal to.

"Do you want more children?" I asked, nauseated, holding the egg as far away as possible as if it were a bomb. The idea of ingesting it was ludicrous and vaguely obscene; I planned to lob it overboard at the first chance.

"Oh, Gawd, no!" Trisha screamed, and all the children turned to glare at us. "I've closed up the shop, if you know what I mean. This is strictly a hobby now."

"Gross," I heard Frankie Senior mutter, as he turned away, and at that moment I had to side with the kids.

By nine o'clock in the morning, the ocean was a flat, steaming, blue iron. My face was wet and sweat ran in rivulets down my armpits. I sat in a bikini top and cut-offs. Kent used to say that I had kept my figure from high school, that no one would ever guess I was the mother of two. Trisha knotted her top under her breasts, revealing a dull, white, stretch-marked belly. We played about a dozen rounds of gin, and I lost each game. Trisha's initial glee turned to boredom and then concern.

"You've got to have a strategy," she kept saying.

"I like to keep my options open," I said, and then lost that hand, too.

"No point in playing if you don't want to win," she said gently. "Everyone wants to win."

Although we might never be soulmates, I decided I liked her.

Finally, disgusted, Trisha quit playing with me and read fashion magazines instead. I climbed the ladder to join the men.

On top was another world, and I pinched Kent hard on his side, angry that he hadn't thought to share this with me sooner.

"Some Superman you are."

I don't want to get misty-eyed, but I might even concede to Kent that it was Life-Altering, at least in the fact that for those few minutes I forgot my small miserable self and just lived out there on the water. It was the first time in a long time that I felt truly free. I can't explain it any other way, but that it's the unthinkable shock of losing happiness.

When the kids were still in high-chairs, refusing to eat, we devised a game: Kent became Superman, I became Lois Lane. Eventually Hunter wanted to be Superboy, and Isabel chose Supergirl. When we adopted a Labrador from the pound, he had no choice but to become Krypto the Superdog. We even had a secret handshake, curling the index finger and hooking them together to form links. When we stood in a circle holding hands this way, we were invincible.

On the boat, staring out at the water, I noticed that all three of us—Kent, Captain Bob, and I—had these goofy smiles on our faces, but I didn't care.

At first we were simply passing the floating buoy platforms that marked the channel. Seals clustered on the narrow ledge, bobbing and barking, seeming to enjoy the day as much as we were.

I called down the ladder, "Trisha, kids, take a look at the seals," but all I got back was a weak, "Great."

A half-hour later, the first silvered crescent of dolphin rose from the waves. Captain Bob pulled a hard turn to follow him, the ship tilting, but luckily Kent and I had the advantage of being prepared for the turn, bracing ourselves in our seats.

Down below, they did not fare as well. We heard dull thuds, the bleating call of one of the children.

"What the heck's going on up there?" Dick yelled up.

"Dolphin," Captain Bob said.

There was a sigh and then Dick started up the ladder. "I thought this was a shark trip."

"The sea's a capricious mistress," Captain Bob said, pulling on the throttle and gunning after the dolphins.

At first there was only the one, but then another jumped up, and they ribboned around each other, until another five joined in. They shuddered and sparkled and flipped in the sun, and then there were twenty, then fifty—I jumped up and down clapping, we were riding herd—then the number multiplied to maybe a hundred, crashing down the wide open plain of the ocean. I had forgotten what a miracle the world was. Behind me, I heard Dick pop two beer cans, then he and Kent sat and talked.

"So what do you do in the real world?" Kent asked.

I snorted and rolled my eyes at Captain Bob. How could these heathens sit drinking brewskis and talking shop? It occurred to me in a moment of self-pitying insight that I was married to a man who no longer understood me. Never mind that each time he held my hand I recoiled. How could I try again when I had proved myself unable to protect? Captain Bob seemed to intuit all this—at least the dull glow in his little brown eyes made him look like he did. I think he could sniff out despair in another person like it was stale sweat, so intimately acquainted he appeared to be with misfortune. He winked.

"How about a puff of Mexican gold?" he whispered. "Then this dolphin shit will blow your mind wide open."

"Why not?" I said. Why not, indeed? Who was I to play the role of moral compass on this boat, to tell the kids to eat vegetables and wear sunscreen and watch the damn miracle of fish out there on the water because life was fleeting? *No mia problema.*

"I sell bull sperm," Dick said, and Kent snorted out about a thimbleful of beer through his nostrils. "No!"

"Yes."

"No kidding?"

"International operation," Dick said, nodding. "We prep 'em, tube 'em, Fedex in dry ice all over the world."

"There's money in that?" Kent said.

"You couldn't guess. Europe's bulls have a low count. Not enough calves being born. In China, the bulls are just not interested. Scientific know-how to the rescue."

"Amazing."

"Pays for these little junkets. And a cabin up at Tahoe."

"Gotta hand it to you," Kent said.

"Just wear a glove," Dick answered, and they both laughed uproariously, past the point of being able to breathe, like they were some comedy team, some rat-pack fraternity or something. I didn't even recognize my husband.

Captain Bob tugged on my arm and pointed to one of the last, laggard dolphins, far behind the rest of the school. His head broke through the waves but then his trajectory was broken, and he was yanked back under. Captain Bob pressed a big red button like you'd see on a game show, and a bell started clanging like crazy while he shouted, "Shark, shark! Get your line."

The day broke in half then, what came after like another life compared to what came before.

Dick hurtled down the ladder, nearly breaking his neck in the process, to retrieve his line. Captain Bob cut the engine and yelled down to Sally to dump out the chum bucket. Stoned, I stretched out on the vacated banquette after Kent climbed down to watch the excitement.

From my vantage point, the water at the end of the boat looked like a bloody sewer—fish parts and blood purpling in the blue. Suddenly a black shadow passed through the blood, like a submarine coming to the surface, and then there was a dead whiteness as the head of the shark appeared above water, feeding on fish parts. I turned away, a chill running through me despite the hot day, grim reaper, as Dick yelled that the shark had grabbed his line.

It seemed like lifetimes—the shrieking of the line as it unspooled, the screaming of directions, first from Captain Bob as he maneuvered the boat around, then Sally, yelling in his thick Spanish accent, "*Tira, tira.* Let her run." Finally he stood behind Dick in an awkward embrace and helped him hold the bowing rod.

I looked out the other direction, but the sea was empty, the flight of the dolphins a memory.

When the catch surfaced the first time, big surprise, no shark. Rude guest, he must have eaten chum and run, chasing after the delectable dolphins. At first, Sally thought they had hooked a sailfish or marlin from the looks of the prehistoric fan along the back, but the second time it surfaced we all saw the golden-yellow body of a dorado.

Captain Bob, satisfied, returned to his captain's chair and opened another beer. "At least no one's going to lose a leg today," he said.

"What?" I said.

"Sharks are sadists."

The lack of movement made the air a heavy wet sheet against the skin. Reluctantly I climbed down to use the galley bathroom, wash my face with fresh water, or, better yet, take a cold shower.

They had reeled the exhausted fish alongside the boat, and Sally was hanging over, hooked under the railing by his ankles, swinging the gaff and plunging it into the fish's gills. Kent looked on, his face tight with a blend of admiration and envy and maybe bloodlust. I hurried inside and locked myself in the bathroom. After I had stalled as long as humanly possible, I peeked out the door. It was quiet, Trisha and the kids standing in the doorway, looking out at the deck. Show over.

I walked over to join them and stopped in my tracks. It was like a piece of the sun had been torn away and laid on our grimy deck—the body as big as me, weighing at least a hundred pounds. A flutter of blood pulsed down the torn gills, and I averted my eyes, intending to escape back up the ladder, but the only way to reach it was to walk around the hulking body. I tiptoed, as if it were asleep, or rather, as if it was one of those monsters in a horror movie that might reach out and grab my foot, swallowing me whole. As I passed the head, I looked down into its eye that was not like an eye at all, but more like a magic button, reflective and complex, promising to transport you like in one of those fairytales to an alternate place. Just as I set my hand on the ladder railing, Trisha screamed, and I turned to see a wild flex of the fish's body, like a giant muscle, a fist, crushing. Sally ran and pulled out a shortened baseball bat, and I stood, sickened and transfixed, as he delivered a fatal thud to the head. The fish's body spread and uncoiled, and I realized, stricken, that it had been alive when I looked into its eye and saw only object, not living thing. Me, the last thing to register in its fishy brain.

"Can I hit it?" came the thin, wheedling voice of Frankie Junior, who had hardly been heard that day.

"Sure," Sally said with a big grin, and the pink, round, avid little boy hurried forward.

Frankie Senior frowned, and Sally waved him over, too, handing him the gaff, and both boys fell on the gold body.

"That's a beauty," Captain Bob sighed. "Don't see dorado that big anymore."

"It was fun, but it wasn't a shark," Dick said.

"Shark's a serious fish. Got to have the stomach for it."

"I really wanted to try for a marlin," Kent said, to no one in particular.

Everyone stood around watching the brutal, rosy boys go to town on the fish. I closed my eyes, thinking I was hallucinating, that my imagination was over-heated as Kent now always chided me, that the revulsion I felt could be thought away. I felt the acid contents of my stomach against the back of my teeth. I looked over at placid Betsy and saw the wet stain on her khaki shorts where she had peed herself.

In a lunge, I straddled the defeated fish and ripped the bat out of Frankie Junior's hand. I boomeranged it over the side, far out over the water. I tore away the gaff from Frankie Senior, even as he tugged on it for dear life, and flung it over as well.

"It's not your right," Frankie Senior said, narrowing his eyes till they disappeared in pillows of flesh.

I took him by the shoulders and shook him, knowing all the while that everything that mattered had already happened, that my actions were worse than ineffectual.

"Monster," I said. "You're a little monster."

The adults sprang to action. Kent grabbed me; Dick and Trisha herded the kids together.

"Don't ever touch my child! You're the monster," Trisha yelled, her puffed face now livid.

We motored back to the harbor—Kent and I huddled on top with Captain Bob, the Hornbergs camped in the galley. Alone on the deck, Sally gutted and cleaned the fish.

"I don't believe in taking women or children to battle. It's a man's sport," Captain Bob muttered to himself.

Once we tied up, the Hornbergs stood on the dock as Sally handed over bags of the packaged dorado.

Captain Bob said nothing but gave me a long hug. Tears welled up in my eyes.

"I have that effect on most women," he said.

We stalled, but the Hornbergs kept standing by the boat like a final hazing, and finally we had to climb down and walk past them to leave.

"Here," Dick said, thrusting out a bag of the fish.

"Thanks," Kent said.

"Sorry," I croaked out as Kent poked me hard in the ribs.

"Forget it happened," Trisha said. "We all just got a little... emotional with all the excitement."

"Yeah." I wondered if this whitewashing of the unpleasant worked for her, and if it did, why couldn't I seem to manage it? It was probably easier than Prozac.

The truth was however I tried to dislike the Hornbergs in the particular, I envied them in the universal—they were a ring of curled index fingers.

They, not we, were a family.

They started to move off, the children's eyes shy and averted. I looked at the back of Betsy's head, willing her to turn and smile, wondering why she didn't see I had done it for both of us.

"By the way," Trisha called back, "happy anniversary."

I flinched as if I had been clubbed. Kent put one arm around me and carried the bag of fish in the other. Kent, Superman after all, had let the Hornbergs go on despising us. He knew I'd rather come off as a jerk than be forgiven by trading on our tragedy. I saw the possibility of grace for us.

Back in our hotel room, I undressed to shower off the salt from my skin. I picked up the framed photo of Isabel and Hunter sitting in front of a Christmas tree, and put it away, face down, in a drawer. I no longer needed to see the picture because it would forever be behind my eyelids each time I closed them.

Alone, Kent walked down the streets of the town and gave the bag of fish to the first young boy he could find with hunger in his eyes.

Hadn't the fish looked like the sun lying on that grimy deck, like a puddle of pure molten gold?

EXCERPT FROM

SPOON MOUNTAIN OR BUST

BY JOHN NICHOLS

*A man's reach should exceed his grasp
or what's a mountain for?*

Forty-eight hours after my visit to the emergency room, I decided to climb Spoon Mountain on my sixty-fifth birthday in three weeks. I'm not saying that's the smartest idea I ever had in my life, but I've always been a stubborn case. I'm a novelist, I write screenplays, I'm an athlete, I've been married three times, I can live with pain. I wanted to climb that mountain on my birthday with my children, Ben and Miranda. But they were not pleased at the prospect.

Ben said, "I don't think you should be climbing mountains right now, Pop. You don't look so hot to me."

Ben was thirty-eight, he weighed two-ten and measured six-two. He had a square jaw, a crew cut, and hooked to his belt were a Leatherman, a tape measure, and a Nokia cell phone.

He added, "How high is Spoon Mountain anyway?"

I told him. "Twelve thousand nine hundred and ninety-nine feet."

"You're kidding." He blanched.

I said, "Ben, I need to show you and Miranda where to scatter my ashes. We'll have fun. It'll be a gorgeous day. Maybe we'll see a bighorn sheep. You will remember it forever."

Ben said, "I don't want to scatter your ashes, Pop, you're not going to die. Calm down, you're tripping out. How much did you have to drink?"

Then he hung up and promptly called Miranda in the Capital City three hours south, and four seconds later Miranda dialed me to read me a riot act.

"What do you mean you're going to climb Spoon Mountain on your birthday in three weeks? Have you gone completely mental, Dad? Ben says you went to the ER because you thought you were having a heart attack."

"No way." I explained to her carefully, "It was a minor case of indigestion that segued into a teensy panic attack compounded by excruciating abdominal spasms due to gas. In short, I ate something that didn't agree with me. A false alarm."

"I don't believe it for a minute," Miranda said. "You always lie about everything. You live in denial."

I said, "I'm scared if we don't do it right now we'll never climb that mountain at all."

"What do you mean 'we,' white man?" she interrupted. "Maybe I'm not tracking this correctly but if my memory serves, I believe you have an annuloplasty ring in your mitral valve; you fluctuate in and out of serious atrial fibrillation on a daily basis despite all the Lanoxin and Coumadin you ingest; you can't walk straight because of the oscillopsia; and when was the last asthma attack that floored you— six weeks ago? And that's merely for starters. I feel as if I'm listening to a quadriplegic inform me he's planning to dance the Lambada all night with Charo."

My girlfriend, Sally Trevino, is almost fifty. She has three teenage boys, Alex, Zachary, and Jason—typical adolescent Neanderthals who believe that *Kill Bill,* a film by Quentin Tarantino, is "awesome." She had them in her thirties. Her ex-husband, Don the Man, despite the restraining order, is probably lurking with an ax as I write in Sally's garage, his yuppie Rasta hairdo positively crackling from jealousy. Although they've been divorced eight years, Don is one of those Deep South cracker backhoe jockies who doesn't get it. On the Plaza once, I saw him use a public garbage can to bash out the windshield of Sally's Isuzu Trooper. When two cops arrived eager to discourage this erratic behavior, Don performed a full-speed headbutt into their cruiser's front grille and wound up undergoing brain surgery for a subdural hematoma.

Sally also has the same kind of mouth as Miranda,
except she is the Latina version:

"*Híjole!* Grow up, *nene*, are you crazy? Are your children
supposed to carry you up that mountain piggyback? Or are
you planning to rent a motorized high-altitude wheelchair?
I can picture you locked in atrial fibrillation above the
timber line facing hurricane-force winds. You must be out
of your mind."

I explained, "I really need to climb that mountain with
my kids. I've been a terrible father. I don't want to die
without doing something remarkable and important for
them that they can cherish forever."

"So take them to Disneyland, idiot. *You went to the
emergency room.* You could sunbathe on a beach in Hawaii,
for Pete's sake. Or have fun at Branson, Missouri, attending
the Grand Country Music Hall."

"You don't understand," I said.

"Oh yeah? Well, if you really want to commit suicide, I
know an easier way. Call Don the Man on his cell phone,
I'll give you the number, and tell him we screw each other.
He will go postal, *te lo juro.* The top of his head will fly
all the way to the moon and back. We're not talking here
about a sentient human being. Don has two assault rifles, a
shotgun, eight pairs of Chuck Norris nunchucks and a can
of pepper spray. He will pry open your jaws with a crowbar
and shove his sneaker down your throat. It'd be way more
fun than dying on a mountaintop."

A couple of days later, Miranda left a message on my
answering machine:

"Hi, Papa-san, are you still alive? How come my phone
isn't ringing with you on the other end? If you don't contact
us toot sweet, Michael and me and Rachel will drive up
there in person and kick your booty big time."

I reached her on the sixth floor pediatrics ICU of
University Hospital where she was caretaking a five-year-
old girl attached to life support after being wounded by
a ricochet from a drive-by shooting. Miranda is thirty-

four, she has one child, Rachel, who starts kindergarten next fall.

"I worry when you don't call," my daughter said. "How's the old sump pump functioning? Are you taking your Lanoxin? Are you eating properly?"

"I eat great," I lied, surreptitiously chewing on a Kit-Kat whose glucose overload was probably maiming my pancreas. "Each night I consult the Dean Ornish heart-friendly cookbook to rustle up another magical repast that eliminates bad cholesterol, lowers my blood pressure, scrubs all the plaque from my arteries, and makes my turds wheat-colored and buoyant in the bowl."

"Don't be a wise guy, Dad. I recruited Ben and Jamie to cook you a special buffalo meat and blueberries stew that I sent them the recipe for. You need protein and plenty of anti-oxidants."

"Buffalo meat and *blueberries?*"

"And tomorrow you should receive from me Priority Express a carton of vitamins that you have to take daily or I'm not climbing with you. Folic acid and magnesium, a box of those Emergen-C packets, B-12 and ginkgo biloba. Are you eating a banana every day? You need the potassium."

"I eat two bananas every morning," I said, opening another Kit-Kat and demolishing half of it with one chomp. I used to play ice hockey and tennis before the oscillopsia hit. I danced across boulders while fishing the Rio Grande. I could make love all night without using Viagra.

Miranda ignored my hyperbole, she always does.

"If you don't eat proper including those vitamins, Dad, nobody will climb that mountain with you. Not on our watch will you commit suicide on your sixty-fifth birthday if we can help it. Sixty-five is not thirty-five, hotshot."

"'Suicide?' We're just taking a hike," I protested. "Relax. I climbed Spoon Mountain a hundred times when I was younger. It's a molehill. Going back up will be an important statement."

"A statement? Like what? Like when you exited open heart surgery eleven years ago—remember that? If not, let me refresh your memory. You were frozen blue and inflated like a balloon. Your features were unrecognizable. You had a breathing tube down your throat, a catheter up your penis, and IV needles stuck in both your arms, which were strapped to the gurney at the wrists. I couldn't stop crying for hours. Ben went into the bathroom and upchucked. Even your ravishing teenybopper wife peed in her thong panties and had to be sedated with three Valiums and a Percodan. We don't need that kind of statement in this family ever again."

I really hate telephones, but I can't stop answering them. Maybe it will be my New York agent, maybe a Hollywood producer, maybe some college offering me fifteen hundred bucks for a speech about turning novels into films, and I'm not proud anymore, I'll take it.

"Can I come over, baby? I'm going off my rocker. I won't stay long, Scout's honor."

Politely I said, "Maybe another time, Sally. I'm trying to kick back and mellow out for a change. It's part of 'getting in shape' for Spoon Mountain. Right now I'm sitting outside paying attention to the flowers. You wouldn't understand or be interested. I used to be so close to nature and then I sloughed off in the last few years. I got lazy. Now I'm going back before it's too late. We all have to or it's curtains."

"What do you mean I 'wouldn't understand'? Speak for yourself, *nene*. I have a brain too, in case you hadn't noticed. We'll mellow out together. I'll bring champagne. A few minutes with me won't kill you, I just need a hug. You won't believe what has happened the last few days. I had the whole Mandelman deal locked up, signed, sealed, you name it. I mean creative financing like you never saw before in your life. Half of it from the mortgage company, half from the bank, and sixty thousand held by the seller with a 20K balloon payment every two years, and the transaction fell apart at closing because the buyers decided to get divorced. Excuse me? Am I hearing correctly? Yes, they started bickering right in front of all of us at the title company, she called him a geek, he called her a flaming bitch, and they both walked out. It cost me a 15 K commission and that's not the half of it. Zachary was busted for shoplifting a Tupac CD at Wal-Mart two days ago, and Alex announced last night at dinner that he intends to quit high school his final semester. When I asked 'Why?' he said, 'Cause I'm bored.' You know what his dad said? 'Go for it, Alex.' Where does that pendejo get *his* priorities? We also have another budding crisis situation at home. Jason, who has possessed his driver's license for all of two hair-raising weeks, had a fender bender in the Furr's lot on Saturday with Magistrate Judge Herrera's grandmother. And I had one more deal that bit the dust late yesterday when the buyer, this spastic kook from Lubbock, discovered there's asbestos poisoning the ceiling. Asbestos? I didn't know that. He hired Max Gonzales to do a separate private inspection, and Max is always undercutting my people because I wouldn't do his woody in a backseat five years ago during the Lawrence Festival. You think your schtik is ditsy, *amor*, you ought to try selling property in this market to the crowd that wants it and can afford to pay the outrageously inflated prices."

"Okay," I said glumly. "I guess."

"Okay, what?"

"Okay, I guess you can come over here, Sally. I mean, I couldn't stop you if I wanted to, could I?"

"Should I bring my ice ax and my pitons?" she giggled.

Obediently, I opened the bottle of Freixenet Sally brought and poured two glasses. I was pissed, however. How come I always get in too deep with sexy women who drive me batshit? I lugged another white plastic chair outside, planting it beside my own chair in front of the small flower garden underneath my kitchen window. La Novia nibbled my earlobe, then settled langorously beside me gazing at the bright red poppies, the happy daisies, the irises about to bloom. The day was hot and smoggy, you could smell the statewide forest fires burning out of control. That made me wonder: When would the feds close down the local wilderness because of fire danger caused by the drought? Sally had on a tight blue long-sleeved jersey to die for and beige short shorts and sandals: some cookie. We clinked our glasses. "Here's lookin' at you, kid." Sally torched a doobie and took a puff, but I declined because I was "in training," paying rapt attention to three elm beetles negotiating the hairs of poppy sepals, and to a white-lined sphinx moth buzzing at the phlox while nearby a small black weevil sawed through a wild sunflower twig with its vicious little proboscis.

Zen and the art of insect watching.

My girlfriend grew restless. She said, "This is dumb," and squibbed the cell phone from her pocket and stared at it, hoping to telepathically make it tootle.

I smiled, saying, "Please put that thing away, sweetie, okay?"

Sally said, "No, sweetie, this is my livelihood, it saves me."

I quit smiling and said, "I hate that cell phone, okay?"

She said, "No, not 'okay,' unless you intend to marry me and adopt my three teenage progeny and commit to paying their health insurance, upcoming college tuitions, and car payments, also."

Good point. I stifled, shifting my gaze to some ants milking aphids on the stem of a rosehip bush.

Sally said, "You hate me, don't you? I know you despise my job and my value system. Well, why not? Frankly, I do too. Selling real estate is like balling morbidly fat meat bombs for peanuts at a Shriner's convention, but how else can I make my nut for the kids so they can grow up big and healthy enough to flunk out of college and become cocaine addicts like their father? You're only in it for the sex with me, aren't you?"

"Of course I really love the sex," I admitted. "But I also like—"

Her cell phone bleeped obnoxiously:

"Listen, Gilbert, listen up carefully," Sally said. "I'm only going to say this once because it's after office hours and I'm enjoying myself on an adventure in wild nature. Linda told me there are two covenants on the land, only two. The buyers cannot build until they pay the second balloon in 2005 and own the property outright. And they cannot put a commercial business on it that would affect the residential neighborhood. Also, the present title company won't insure the right-of-way. Black Dog Surveying is researching that problem. The Johnsons won't sign an easement? I think that's bogus posturing. The road has to be public domain. Now if you'll excuse me, I have to commune with the larger cosmos. *Adiós, muchito.*"

I said, "I'll bet there isn't a cell phone on top of Spoon Mountain, what do you think?"

"I honestly don't care what isn't on top of that peak, *querido*. Although for your sake if you reach the summit I hope there is a McDonald's there that only serves Bighorn McNuggets."

A fat raven perched on a nearby Chinese elm branch gabbled and quorked a few times, and I croaked and clucked right back at it, doing okay on the deep throat rattles but not so good on the aspirate H because I was furious at Sally, who rolled her eyes to the sky—*oh spare me, homes!*—and then bussed me lasciviously right on the mouth.

At that precise moment, out the corner of my eye, I noticed Don the Man's tulip red extended-cab Ford pickup slowing for the speed hump on Valverde as Don did a double take . . . and then he peeled away in a real hissy fit.

Next thing I knew, son Ben and his girlfriend Jamie appeared on my kitchen stoop carrying a cardboard box that held ten plastic yogurt containers full of buffalo-meat stew that had masking tape labels on the lids indicating the date I should consume their contents right up until my birthday. Ben's dog Cudjo leaped from the truck bed and chased my cats Cookie and Carlos up a tree, then he flounced into the kitchen and devoured all the cat food. I almost pasted the hound yet restrained myself. Ben was always in too much of a hurry to waste time lollygagging, but Jamie insisted on hanging around for a moment to give me directions.

"All you have to do is thaw a carton and dump the stew into a pot and ignite a burner. One jar equals one meal. Remove it from the freezer when you awaken. Are you drinking plenty of soy milk?"

"What is this goulash made of?" I asked, inspecting a container, aghast. Ben had on his usual construction duds and Jamie looked extra cute in bleached 501 jeans, a gray sweatshirt, and a spiffy blue beret.

"It has lentils, carrots, tofu, celery, onions, garlic, basil, sea salt, free-range buffalo meat from South Dakota that I found at the co-op, and blueberries from Maine. The blueberries are rich in anti-oxidants. All the ingredients are organic."

I said, "Wow. I bet this stuff is delicious."

Ben said, "Don't hustle us, Pop. You have to eat it even if you hate it. Did you get the vitamins Miranda sent?"

I swung open a cabinet door above the sink and gestured at the shiny new bottles in a pretty row: "*Voilà.*"

Ben unsheathed his Leatherman, flicked forth the knife blade, reached up, and one by one slowly and sarcastically cut off the plastic safety wrappers around the bottle caps so they could actually be opened.

"You can't let things sit here growing mold, old man. If Miranda tips you're doing that, we won't climb Spoon Mountain with you. Myself, I think you're totally gonzo, but at least you could make a small effort to wise up. Miranda will bring an oxygen bottle and one of those portable battery-operated cardioversion kits on our trek. However, it'd be excellent if we don't have to use them."

While Ben was slicing off plastic wrappers, Jamie had stacked the yogurt cartons in my freezer, then she checked the main refrigerator compartment, which displayed a bag of stale tortillas, four Tecates, and a half cantaloupe still wrapped by cellophane, with blotches of green penicillin decorating its orangey pink meat.

"Yuck."

She extricated the cantaloupe, dropping it in a wastebasket under the sink, then directed her scorn toward a nearby tub of Kitty Litter.

"Do you ever empty this cat box?"

"Sometimes I forget for a few days," I admitted, eager to expel them before they discovered some reason to ditch Spoon Mountain and commit me to the Living Center over behind Holy Cross Hospital. Surprise visitors to my raunchy digs are never exactly welcome, least of all family members, especially female family members who tend to disapprove of my somewhat—shall we say casual?—housekeeping.

"'A few days?'" Jamie removed her beret and scratched her russet locks. "It looks to me as if your cats have been piling their excrement in that litter unabated for a year."

"Thank you, thank you for all the wonderful food," I said, guiding them firmly toward the kitchen door.

"It's not enough to thank us," Ben cast back over one shoulder as they headed for his truck. "Remember, you have to eat it, okay?"

I ate it, all right, for lunch the next day, an entire yogurt container of free-range buffalo-meat stew teeming with anti-oxidants. The concoction tasted delicious, very spicy. Then everything went wrong behind my abdominal wall, and I spent the next two hours scooting back and forth to the bathroom plagued by a virulent diarrhea. Naturally, my heart clicked into A-fib, and I couldn't get it out with the Valsalva maneuver. Too bad. I had an engagement to perform at my pal Zolofsky's little bookshop, I have fans, I never disappoint them even if only for a hundred bucks paid under the table, not at this late stage of my career. So, dying or not, that's where I went.

Breathless, I dashed into the venue twenty minutes late still unable to exit A-fib. Zolofsky, a large hulking bald man, roared, "The Titanic arrives!" Shirley, his nearly blind assistant (and girlfriend), hugged me raptly, almost tipping me over. Sally said, "¿Qué pasó? You're all pale. Oh no, here we go again." The twenty-five impatient audience members conferred a standing ovation except for Roberto Salazar, who catcalled, "Where's the beard? Where's the guitar?" John Wayne Dahmer, the black Persian tomcat dozing beside the computer monitor at the register, never woke up. "I was about to notify the gendarmes and file a missing persons," Zolofsky said.

I asked Aaron, "Can I use the office and put my feet up for thirty seconds? My heart is having a senior moment."

"Yeah, sure, go for it."

"Wait a minute, stop this show—he's killing himself," Sally protested. "He's no good to me as a cadaver."

"It's okay, I'll be right back," I told the multitudes. "I need to flush a fetus down the toilet."

Roberto Salazar cried, "I'm here to heckle your ugly bones because you never return my phone calls!"

In the office I drank half a bottle of water, lay on my back on the concrete floor, and hooked my heels up over the edge of Aaron's desk. Same old, same old—my heart has been weird for decades. But I'll admit I was a trifle scared. Remember: Sixty-five is not thirty-five, hotshot. And denied sufficient oxygen, the corpuscles of my body were excreting pre-epileptic nausea enzymes, and tinnitus in both ears buzzed loudly. Sally looked ravishing in a low-cut lavender blouse, lemon-yellow slacks, and pink sandals. The owners hovered, squinting at me, who lately had been picturing myself dead, swollen and noisome on the rug by my bed with many bumpy clumps of blowfly larvae wriggling beneath my rotting skin. I understand nobody lives forever, yet I still didn't want to die like that—not now, or at least not before I had achieved the unblemished summit of Spoon Mountain with my kids and done my little dance of exaltation on probably the only spot of earth left in our county untrammeled by human ingenuity.

Aaron said, "Are you okay? Should we call an ambulance? Do you want a cookie?"

"Sure, a cookie would be super," Sally said. "Do you have one with a pound of sugar in it? And maybe a B & B chaser? He wants to be miserable, let's help him out."

Zolofsky ignored the sarcasm. "He looks awful."

Sally muttered, "You ain't seen nothin' yet. Baby, let me take you home, I'll make chicken soup, this isn't worth it.

You're crazy to think about climbing Spoon Mountain on your birthday."

Shirley said, "He couldn't manage a ladder to our attic, let alone Spoon Mountain on his birthday."

That roused my dander. "How much do you want to bet?"

I righted myself, losing my balance, and dived headfirst into the wall, staggering backwards surrounded by cuckoos, dust briffits, and twirling spurls.

"A million bucks," Sally wagered. "This is your idea of 'kicking back and mellowing out'?" To Zolofsky she complained, "Ever since he decided to scale that mountain I can't get through to him at all."

Ferociously, fighting back tears of frustration, I tore open my knapsack, extracted the ratty beard, hooked it on despite a broken tong, buttoned up my grubby Civil War jacket, took a puff off the asthma inhaler, and adopted my booming Walt Whitman persona as I stumbled out front prepared to recite from *Song of Myself*. Walt is one of my alter egos whenever I get bored of reading from my own work. Instead of rhymes by The Great Gray Poet, however, a bunch of banal, chirpy words issued at an almost falsetto pitch from my constricted gullet:

"Hi there, everyone, thanks for your marvelous patience. You folks are angels. I'm sorry I was late, but guess what? In eight days, I'm going to be sixty-five years old, and to celebrate I intend to climb a pretty tall mountain where I expect I'll find—"

And that's when Don the Man lunged through Zolofsky's front doorway swinging a baseball bat. John Wayne Dahmer went flying when the bat crashed against the cash register. Blind Shirley shrieked, Zolofsky cried *"Wait a minute!"* and audience members scattered to avoid the mayhem. More or less used to these scenes, Sally glommed onto the nearest weapon (a ceramic Mexican vase holding fresh-cut zinnias) just as the baseball bat met (and demolished) my lectern (*and* my right forearm raised to deflect the blow), and she beaned her ex-hubby with the vase as Zolofsky and another patron, Gilbert Romero, struck Don with metal folding chairs and he barged into a book rack that fell with an operatic crash. Zolofsky and Gilbert Romero landed on top of him while Sally bapped 911 on her cell phone and bleated "*Hurry up!*" at the cops. Burly Roberto Salazar joined the pileup wielding his belt, which he wrapped twice around Don's wrists and yanked behind his back in the expert fashion of a seasoned calf roper. By the time Philip Martinez and Eric Thompson arrived, Don had been substantially subdued although he was still snarling random obscenities related to his ex-wife's "*puta* infidelities."

"Lock him up and throw away the key!" Sally brayed as they hustled her ex out to the paddy wagon.

Me? I sat in a corner holding my fractured arm, cursing the fact that I was uninsured and still one week shy of Medicare.

Then I vomited.

Miranda was appalled. "What were you doing to him, Papa-san? Screwing his wife? Calling him a right-wing dirt bag in public? Giving his children copies of the latest porn novel you published? And who's Sally? The last I heard your girlfriend was Rowena."

"They've been divorced for years," I said. A lightweight fiberglass cast extended from an inch below my right elbow to the main knuckles of my hand, protecting the reset ulna. Sally had signed it *Te quiero, güero*; Zolofsky had scribbled *Spoon Mt. or Bust* (then he stiffed me for the hundred-dollar reading fee, the bastard).

"But Don is a volatile misfit on a restraining order," I elaborated. "I don't know what happened or why."

"Like you didn't know what happened or why the day you hit on that starlet, Michelle Grainger, when they were shooting *The Lucky Underdogs*? And her boyfriend, the 'volatile misfit' from the Arena Football League, broke your nose with his shoe? And that humiliating photograph was in *People* magazine the week I graduated from nursing school?"

"I didn't hit on Michelle," I protested, abashed at my own pathos. I've had some tacky things happen in life that I'm not proud of, mostly thanks to working on films. "She hit on me," I said. "However, those days are long gone, ancient history. Lanoxin has usurped my testosterone. I'm almost a eunuch, anymore."

Miranda scoffed, "Nobody's a eunuch anymore, Dad, give me a break. Can you say 'Levitra'? Can you say 'Cialus'? Or are you forgetting already that three months ago I sent you two free sample six packs of Viagra I obtained from my buddy, Dr. Lambert, because you begged me to? Speaking of which, are you taking those vitamins I sent?"

"Every morning and every night without fail," I assured her.

"You're lying. I can hear it in your voice."

"No, I'm not. Give me a break."

"What about that stew Jamie and Ben brought over? Do you like it?"

"Yes, I love the stuff. Sometimes I dump it over steaming brown rice for supper. And for breakfast I often fry the leftovers and fashion a burrito with a tortilla. Maybe I sprinkle on a dab of Tabasco for extra flavor."

Miranda said, "I can't stand it. Your voice is so dripping with mendacity. I know you chucked all those containers into the garbage even before Ben's truck was out of the driveway, didn't you?"

"Are you kidding? Jesus. Ye of so little faith."

"I bought a bunch of Gu packets for our trip up that mountain," she said. "Are you climbing Tecolote Hill every day to get in shape? You better be if you know what's good for you. Are you drinking lots of water?"

"Absolutely. What do you take me for, a slacker? I'm an athlete and this is a serious endeavor."

"You used to be an athlete, Dad, before three wives and thirty girlfriends, twenty years of Hollywood, asthma and heart problems, alcohol and horrible eating habits, arthritis, extreme stress, and chronic lack of sleep cut you down to the size of a crippled church mouse."

"Very funny, Miranda. I can see that your apple didn't fall very far from my tree."

"You think you're immortal but you're not," she insisted. "Just because you've dodged so many bullets in the past doesn't mean that the next one hasn't got your name on it."

I said, "Not being afraid of dying is paramount to human liberation."

She replied, "I hate to say this, Father dear, but you are about forty bricks shy of a load."

"Thanks, sweetie. It's always good to chat with you. Bye bye."

A day later, Sally came over to apologize for Don the Man by hauling my ashes. But she required it to be special and exotic, not a cursory hump made drabber by my dour pad. So off we went in her silver Isuzu Trooper to an adobe trophy McMansion on Blueberry Hill, the second home for a pair of decadent faith-based entrepreneurs from Texas. Sally had the keys.

"He's in real estate; she runs a Fort Worth gallery. This humble joint is on the block because they decided to switch their vacation operation to San Miguel de Allende. They also own condos on Maui and a cottage on Martha's Vineyard. The crime rate here finally discouraged them. This house has been burglarized three times over the last eighteen months and tagged by gangbangers twice."

Talk about conspicuous space. It made me want to weep. This was her idea of romance? Cathedral ceilings were fourteen feet high, the vigas massive, blond, beautiful. Sunlight streamed in through wide floor-to-ceiling thermal-paned windows. The floors were polished oaken slats or Mexican tile with radiant heating underneath. You could have played soccer in the living room watched by five hundred fans. There were ornate Persian rugs, a wide-screen TV, a sophisticated stereo system. A thousand mint-condition, hardback first editions stocked the library shelves. The kitchen, flaunting copper pans and iron kettles hanging off pegs, was a professional chef's paradise. All told it was a spotless operation, from the skylights to the well-tended plants nurtured by a weekly garden service that met seasonal landscaping needs and also took care of the swimming pool, the outdoor Jacuzzi, the indoor hot tub, and the tanning salon.

A sultan-sized, four-poster sleeping barge ruled the master bedroom. It had a thick aluminum-blue quilt the color of mountain bluebirds. The view through panoramic windows incorporated a widescreen landscape comprised of the haze-dimmed Sangre de Cristo range from Arroyo Verde to Boulder Peak casting shadows across our town. Spoon Mountain occupied the exact middle of the smoggy picture—flanked by Gavilan and Cabrito peaks—its nipple-shaped nub of a summit sloping gently south along a ridge to the Catherine Lake Overlook.

I'll admit, I was stunned by the difference between this immaculate showcase castle and my own diminutive shanty which was basically three tiny rooms measuring seven-hundred square feet full of paperback books, stacks of manuscripts and unanswered mail, and other generic rubble.

"How much are they asking for this monstrosity?" I asked.

"A million 800K. And they'll get it, too."

"Fuck them. Fuck those—"

"I am soooo sorry about Don the Man," Sally interrupted, kissing me passionately.

"That's okay," I whispered back. "God gives, God takes away. It's no big deal."

Sally slid down my torso, kneeling between my legs, and unzipped my fly and pried out the docile iguana, engulfing it between her painted lips with an infinitely sexy tenderness giving me dreamy head like a Renaissance artist painting the summer clouds above Holland.

Dreedle eep bleep tweet.

The call to Sally was from Chip. "Don't go away," she murmured to me, then explained to Chip: "Chip, it's a commercial building in an attractive location. It can easily be divided into four or five spaces with at least two rentable apartments or more if you wanted. Because of the photo lab in there six years ago, tests will have to be done to make sure there's no toxic residue, you can't avoid that. Irregardless, given the possible future earnings and the great location, two and a quarter is a weak listing. I wouldn't commence with anything lower than two-fifty. If you're willing to carry the paper or wind up having to carry it, you can ask for more. I'd stake my license on it. *Ciao, bello.*"

But I couldn't get into it. I was as wilted as Free Willie's dorsal fin. Truth to tell, except for Ben and Miranda, I felt all alone on earth, also mega-depressed, and I wanted to cry for help, except that would blow my cover and sound foolish, wouldn't it? You live by the sword you die by the sword, I always say. That cliché is in every book I've published.

"What's wrong, *mi alma?*" Sally asked, alarmed, cupping the poor destitute thing between her delicate palms like a flickering votive candle. "Now you don't love me anymore?" She glanced up at my eyes and, reacting to their gaze, turned her head to look out the picture window toward what I was staring at.

"Oh, *chulo,*" she cried. "*That mountain is destroying our relationship.*"

Yes, of course the Floresta shut down the National Forest because of the fire danger, God damn their eyes. Six days shy of my birthday. I reread the announcement twice. All of the National Forest or almost all anyway. That meant half the county was now out of bounds, and the fines for trespassing could be up to five thousand dollars. *Five thousand dollars? ¡Híjole!* Even Tecolote Hill, my training path at the mouth of Sierra Canyon, was CLOSED DUE TO EXTREME FIRE DANGER. *Assholes.* In fact, the only "local" trail left open as a sop to tourists was the well-beaten track to Gallegos Lake in the wilderness area, but everywhere beyond the lake had been declared off limits, including Gavilan Peak and Spoon Mountain. After my first blush of outrage, I decided: So what? Screw the feds. I don't care. *Up against the wall, Smokey, black power's gonna get your momma!* "Nobody but nobody stops me from my appointed rounds on my sixty-fifth birthday." If this was a foolish declaration, so what? Hadn't I spent a lifetime, against all odds, publishing books and writing screenplays? Let alone surviving heart problems, debilitating asthma, dysfunctional relationships? Face it, I've always been a mensch. That meant that a few days from now, Ben and Miranda and I were going to easily break the law by climbing Spoon Mountain because the Forest Service had only ten rangers to patrol five-hundred-thousand square miles, hence they could never in their wildest dreams catch yours truly and my progeny who would be transformed by then into your basic Marxist-Leninist eco-liberation invisible needles in a haystack: *We'll wear cammy outfits and oak-leaf tundra netting to outfox those inept government flunkies patrolling the ridges with their noisy helicopters*—

Later that day around dusk, I was driving home after warming up for Spoon Mountain by illegally climbing Tecolote Hill once again. Resist much, obey little. Though I had been nervous the entire time, nobody had cited me for breaking the law, I was too sly, too clever, too surreptitious, a fleeting shadow on the land, also a desperate man who would kill you with a single karate chop if you were meshuga enough to attempt an arrest before next Monday, you dumb fuck. *I mean it.* A murky sky stretched away, smoke pollution almost obliterating Boulder Peak down south, a full moon choking on its own fading luster through the noxious haze. Roast in hell, planet. A flattened skunk lay on the shoulder, beleaguered by a trio of brazen ravens who did not flap away because they knew I wouldn't swerve to hit them. *Au contraire*, through the open window I called "Quork, quork" while chugging by, and one of the birds said "Klok" in return. As I buffed up for Spoon Mountain, conversing with ravens was becoming a whole new reenergized skill highlighting my linguistic devolution away from alphabetized language back toward the saner twittings of birds, bats, bumblebees, and brachiopods. Then a magpie flew across the road and I waved, eliciting a sassy tail flick in return.

It was late and I was sitting at the computer putting the finishing touches on my Library Convention speech, which is scheduled for next month (and will earn me $500.00 and also, unfortunately, a 1099 form), when those scaredy cats Cookie and Carlos scampered through the living room into the bedroom, and at the same moment I heard a terrible crashing sound outside the kitchen door. Oh wonderful. Had Don the Man escaped from the county lockup? Of course anyone could be out there, because all kinds of lunatics dropped by my place at ungodly hours. A total stranger had appeared shortly after eleven one night, beeped his horn, and demanded that I contribute two hundred dollars to the Mumia Abu-Jamal defense fund in Philadelphia. Another guy entered the driveway and fired a pistol toward the sky screaming *"Up yours, you friggin' eco-freak!"* A young woman showed up at four a.m. covered with dust, all messed up on drugs and booze, her lower lip bleeding as she beseeched me for shelter because some wasted *tecatos* were chasing her. When I drove her home to a rattletrap trailer behind Super Wal-Mart, she attempted to borrow twenty bucks, then produced a joint from her pocket and wanted to turn on together, cursing me when I declined. They materialized from the violent night and disappeared back into it. I kept a loaded .22 pistol in my top bureau drawer underneath the socks, but I feared that gun. I had never removed it from the dresser. How could one human being point a weapon at another human being? What did you do, yell "Suck on this!" and then pull the trigger? Yet I inhabited a violent town, I was a controversial public figure, and it was no secret where I lived.

Plus everybody wanted to squash my Spoon Mountain expedition. Who knows, maybe even Ben and Jamie, those incipient Quislings, were outside determined to scare me straight. And I wouldn't have put it past Miranda and Michael to have driven north for the party. Suddenly I snapped and leaped to the top bureau drawer for my .22 pistol. It was time to fight fire with fire, I'm a U.S. American, aren't I? Buck up, you sniveling tub of guts. *Go ahead, make my day.* Then, armed and dangerous (though with a pounding heart), I sneaked across the kitchen to the door and listened. Some kind of type-A aggressive mammal high on methamphetamines picked up the plastic garbage dumpster and again hurled it against the outside wall.

I crouched to one side in case bullets came through the door as I called, "Hey, pal, what are you doing? Are you a brain-dead animal? I'm trying to bag a little shuteye here. *It's three o'clock in the morning!*"

The assailant kicked the dumpster sideways, pummeled it with a big stick or a sledge hammer, and then punched apart sacks of garbage, sounding like an elephant dancing flamenco atop sheets of gigantic bubble wrap.

"Yo, listen up!" I shouted. "I've got a gun in my fist and it's loaded! This isn't funny! Go home! Quit drinking. Who are you?"

For an answer, the dumpster was vigorously punted against the wall once again, obviously the work of more than one person, say the disrespectful juvenile delinquents from Sally's dysfunctional family—Jason, Zachary, and Alex—bribed by their mom (or their dad) to create an uproar robbing me of sleep, rattling my nerves, and sabotaging my alpine hiking confidence. At this thought, I grew way more irate than I was afraid—*¡basta ya!*—so I grabbed a flashlight from a basket on the sideboard and rashly unlocked the door.

"*I have a gun you bastards and I'm coming out!*" I clicked on my flashlight, cocked the double action six-shot Harrington & Richardson model 649 revolver in my left hand, and jerked open the door, fully prepared to execute the interlopers.

A single bear froze, caught by the flashlight's beam. Or sort of a bear, anyway, missing half one ear, with much of its fur matted or crusted by blood or snot or by rotting gobs of free-range organic buffalo-meat stew rich in anti-oxidants, and it probably weighed less than a hundred and fifty pounds. It was seated eight feet away beside the overturned dumpster, surrounded by a pile of shredded paper and plastic yogurt containers and other rubbish, a week's accumulation because collection day was tomorrow. Over my entire life I had seen only a trio of wild bears, all three spotted from a distance while I was grouse hunting, and they had been departing vertiginously in the opposite direction. This bear was not running in any direction, however. It blinked its beady eyes, or at least one beady eye—the other had been mashed back into the socket. Over the long pointy snout was draped an empty plastic sack that had held frozen peas I had consumed for dinner three nights ago. The bear's posture, with front paws clutched against a furry chest that had a white patch rising bib-like to a ring around the neck, made it appear a tattered yet somehow cuddly teddy bear.

I leveled my cheap pistol at the animal, saying, "Shoo, scat." The bear blinked again, then lifted one paw and plucked the bag off its nose, revealing a scar across the bridge so distinct it could have been made by a hatchet. The gesture also called attention to its claws, which were really large and very sharp. To be polite, I lowered my flashlight beam from the peculiar undersized eye and spoke again:

"Shoo. Scat. Go away from here."

Articles I have read about black bears insist that on ninety-nine percent of encounters they run away from people. Yet this bear had no intention of taking a powder. He (she?) continued to sit there, made punchy by hunger no doubt, its one orb peeping at me while awaiting my next move. This may sound like anthropomorphizing an animal, but I had a sense that our scruffy ursine intruder could have been the mirror image of myself.

And as the seconds blipped along, I not only lost my fear but an unexpected calm smoothed my goose bumps and my aggravated heart quieted a bit. There are moments, even confronted by a blasted wreck like this, when awe is the only proper feedback—i.e., when was the last occasion I had been face to face with something wild and untamed and commensurate to my capacity for wonder? Maybe the poor animal was an emissary from Spoon Mountain urging me not to give up the dream.

I closed my eyes and pinched my nose, taking a deep breath, and when I opened up I actually brushed aside two tears.

"Get out of here," I whispered gently to that fellow traveler. "They really will waste you if you stick around any longer."

No deal. I'm not leaving. And in this drought where can I go anyway?

Okay, I aimed my pistol at the sky and fired a cheerful, non-threatening, goodbye-my-friend warning shot, an act that elicited immediate response. Fast as a chickadee, Scarface dropped to all fours, pivoted, and bolted smack against the side of the empty dumpster—blonk!—and with a strangled huff of panic then backed away among the scattered refuse heaps, whirled, and, obviously confused, charged directly at me, dumping me flat on my butt and catching its teeth against my left pant leg as I rolled off the stoop toward a patch of weeds. The pant leg ripped open right up the seam to my belt as I screamed and banged the bear on its head with my cast. Apparently that hurt, because Scarface hesitated, stunned, blinking that one little eye, then suddenly yelped, sprinted away, and disappeared.

Holy methuselah.

I don't quite know how to explain the logic behind this, but Sally took one look at my left eye swollen shut, and my lopsided nose to go along with the cast on my right arm, and she broke up with me.

"What were you *thinking*?" she accused. She was livid. "Look at you, you are an incredible mess. I'm a business woman, image is everything, how do you suppose you look on my résumé? Two years ago they voted me Realtor of the Year, then I began dating you *y mira to que ha pasado.* My ex-husband, an immature petty tyrant who wants to smash everything in revenge, is cooling his heels in the local hoosegow, and my current *novio* can't stand up in public without getting bashed by a baseball bat or being battered by a bear. I'll admit, I love you with all my heart, but you constantly break my heart. What is the problem, I'm not good enough for you, the genius writer who lost all his money in umpteen divorces? The genius ecologist who can't stop eating mayonnaise and baloney? The genius athlete who falls flat on his face if you poke him with only a feather? What, I'm too tacky? I'm too Chicana? I'm too noisy? I wear too much makeup? My *chichis* are too big? You say you want to bond with your children on top of Spoon Mountain? When are we—you and me!—allowed to bond on a special occasion? Maybe for once in your life will you even say 'I love you' to me? What are you so afraid of? Dating you is like being skewered by a Paul Rodriguez skit ridiculing women, and I deserve better than that. Every time we screw, I feel farther away from you afterwards than when we started. But at least we used to screw. Now I'm living a thousand miles away from you even though I live next door, what is the point of that? Human beings are supposed to love each other, but you act as if emotional proximity is equal to anthrax bacteria. Come to think, now that I reconsider, I've had it, damn you, it's all over between us. Baby, overnight your obsessing on that pinche mountain has made you psychotic even *before* you climbed it!"

Then naturally Miranda says, "Sorry, Charley, you are not climbing Spoon Mountain tomorrow."

I replied, "Yes I am and nobody can stop me."

Ben and Jamie were attending my birthday eve bash along with Michael, Miranda, and Rachel, who were bunking at the Aztec Inn. The shiny four-year-old sprite Rachel was as cute as molasses wearing Mary Janes, a denim halter top, and a Pittsburgh Steelers baseball cap. Michael could have squashed me with one finger: How do the young grow so large and handsome and strong? Miranda is a tall girl with green eyes that always twinkle and an easy, often comical manner. I have long thought of her as the grownup of our family, a gracious level-headed babe, intelligent, the true genetic hope for our line.

We were all crowded around the kitchen table of my prosaic dump, scarfing a repast that Ben and Jamie had contrived, featuring a pot of linguini with mussels and scallops, steamed broccoli, and a salad of arugula, marinated artichoke hearts, and mung bean sprouts accompanied by several bottles of cheap pinot noir, Jamie's favorite vino. Ben's dog Cudjo was snoozing under the table with an ear cocked and one eye open waiting for Cookie or Carlos to blunder inside through the cat door.

"No you're not," Miranda said. "Look at yourself, have you checked a mirror lately? You could be a prisoner that was tortured at Abu Ghraib. Are you blind in that eye? Do you have any idea how ghoulish your face is? Do you know what happens if you perform extreme exercise at high altitudes with all those contusions and broken blood vessels?"

"Doesn't matter," I said. "I'm going."

With an effort, she held her temper. "When you are better, maybe. Why not? But now let's be rational. Twice a week on the Pediatric ICU, I watch children succumb from you wouldn't believe what traumas. Car accidents, domestic cleansers, drug ODs, congenital heart defects. Under the right circumstances, it's really easy for people to die. But if you want to climb that mountain, fine. Only first get back into shape for two months, go on a diet, lose twenty pounds, and then we'll talk turkey after you do a treadmill that says you're game to go, fair enough?"

More than fair. It made perfect sense to me. A prudent strategy at last, thank God.

But I said, "No, we have to do it right now on my birthday. If we don't do it now it'll never be done. I'm tackling that mountain tomorrow with or without you guys."

"No you aren't," Ben said. "And if you insist on going alone, we'll notify the Forest Service that you're breaking the law and they'll post a tactical unit guarding the wilderness boundary at Gallegos Lake all day."

Miranda said, "We're not attacking you, Dad, you're attacking us. Suicide is a very aggressive act against the people who love you the most."

I said, "Suicide, schmuicide. This is important. If it's postponed it will never happen."

"That's not true," Ben said. "Pop, we're not disrespecting you. We love you and we were ready to hike with you until this happened."

I jutted forward my lower lip. "I don't give a hoot, Ben. Tomorrow I climb that mountain."

Miranda said, "My dear old man: You take Lanoxin, you take Coumadin, you're in and out of atrial fibrillation every six minutes, two weeks ago you nearly had a heart attack and wound up in the emergency room, and that mountain is almost thirteen thousand feet high. Ben and I will accompany you when you're healed, but not until. And that's final. Since the heart scare two weeks ago, you've been assaulted by a lunatic and then blindsided by a bear, and your girlfriend dumped you like a bad habit. Your kharma is in a seriously retro phase."

Ben said, "If you try to climb that high on your birthday tomorrow it'll be exactly like every other meltdown in your life."

His sister elaborated: "The best case scenario is an asthma crisis waylays you before the atrial arrhythmia catalyzes ventricular fib or you croak from internal bleeding. Or you are busted—the infamous left-wing writer and environmental do-gooder—for trespassing in a forest closed to hiking because of the fire danger and then it's headlines to shame us on every paper in the state. To shame you on every paper in the state."

"I don't care." I inspected my hands, the cast on my arm. "I am going to summit Spoon Mountain tomorrow. Period. Exclamation point. End of discussion."

They fell silent, eyeing me while I glowered at them sadly . . . and defiantly.

Rachel, a perfect child, was wielding crayons on a Dora the Explorer coloring book. Cudjo snored. Allergic to cats, Jamie sneezed. Miranda blew her nose onto a paper towel and remained calm. "You have to give it up, Dad, no eleventh-hour heroics. Better to eat humble pie. Look at you, you can't even survive at this altitude, let alone at twelve thousand feet." She reached over and playfully tweaked my nose. "We are not climbing that mountain with you tomorrow because we love you too much. I'm sorry, it just isn't right."

"Yes it is," I said.

Miranda stood up and went behind me, leaning to put her arms around me as she pressed her cheek against the side of my wounded head, manipulating, manipulating. "Poppa, we adore you, doesn't that make any impression on your addled bean? You're funny, you're a flake, and you're a beautiful human being. We even respect your ludicrous stubborn behavior against all the odds, because compared to most people at least you have balls. However, we don't want to lose you yet."

I thought about that. I didn't want to lose them either. But we would get nowhere talking about how much we loved each other. The situation demanded a different tack. I was tired of being obtuse. Quietly I said, "I am climbing that mountain tomorrow. And nobody is going to stop me."

My lovely daughter straightened up and took me by surprise. She said, "Okay, Dad. Come on guys. Let's bail on this punk."

"Whoa," Ben said. "Take it easy, Miranda."

"You take it easy, Ben. Come on, everybody, time's up. I'm turning into a pumpkin."

"Oh hey, wait a sec," Michael said. "It's Grampa's birthday. He's sixty-five years old. We didn't come here to—"

"*To hell with Grampa's birthday,*" Miranda said. "Grampa is a moron. I'm sick of Grampa and all his self-righteous bullshit and his lugubrious self-annihilation complex for the last thirty years! I know why he wants to climb Spoon Mountain tomorrow, and I sympathize with his desire, but frankly I don't give a rat's ass if he murders himself doing it because he's in no condition to succeed. Let Ralph Nader speak at his funeral, *I went fishin'.*"

Ben waved his hands. "No no, we can't let it end this way. She apologizes, Pop, she doesn't mean it, do you, Mandy? We love you. Stop. Look. Nobody even finished their food."

"Let *him* finish the food, Ben." Miranda grabbed Rachel, who had dropped her crayons and was frowning darkly. "And I hope he chokes on it. I hope his LDL cholesterol goes through the roof and blows out his arteries tomorrow. Come on, Michael, let's ditch this grubby hole before the sanctimony gives me an aneurism."

"*Wait!*" Ben cried.

"GET OUT OF HERE!" I yelled. "ALL OF YOU!"

Cudjo barked, but Jamie shouted "Shuttup!" so loudly the dog cowered, belly against the floor. Ben had a stunned, heartbroken look, as if he should have been the man in our family who could save everybody with his forceful attitude and wise decisions, thus averting a debacle. Like father like son, but I had news for him—lotsa luck.

"Nobody even finished our food," Ben pleaded. "And what about the cake and ice cream—?"

AN INTERVIEW WITH JOHN NICHOLS

BY GREG FRASER

John Nichols was born in 1940, in Berkeley, California. He attended Hamilton College, in upstate New York, where he played collegiate ice hockey, ran cross country, and started in earnest as a novelist. His first book, *The Sterile Cuckoo*, was published in 1965 and turned into a feature film starring Liza Minnelli and directed by Alan Pakula. Subsequent novels include *The Wizard of Loneliness* (the film version of which features Lukas Haas), *A Ghost in the Music, American Blood, An Elegy for September, Conjugal Bliss: A Comedy of Martial Arts, The Voice of the Butterfly*, and his most recent, *The Empanada Brotherhood*. Nichols is best known for his New Mexico Trilogy, which includes *The Milagro Beanfield War* (made into a major motion picture by Robert Redford), *The Magic Journey*, and *The Nirvana Blues*. The author, as well, of several nonfiction collections such as *On the Mesa, A Fragile Beauty, If Mountains Die, The Last Beautiful Days of Autumn, An American Child Supreme: The Education of a Liberation Ecologist*, and *The Sky's the Limit: A Defense of the Earth*, John Nichols has been described by scholar Peter Wild as a writer whose forte is his "glittering humor" and whose main authorial concerns lie with "how power is used and abused to control people and resources." An accomplished screenwriter, photographer, and cartoonist, as well as an avid hiker, Nichols lives in Taos, New Mexico, his home for the past forty years.

FRASER: You recently donated your archives to the University of New Mexico. What kinds of materials can scholars and students of your work expect to find in this literary repository? Private letters, publishers' contracts, journal writings, drafts of novels?

NICHOLS: My archives going to the University of New Mexico library consist of manuscripts and drafts of manuscripts for almost everything I've written since I was thirteen years old. There are notebooks and handwritten manuscripts of novels I wrote all through college, but never published. There are manuscripts to many short stories, to every speech I've ever given, to every magazine article I've written. There are manuscripts to all the screenplays I wrote for Hollywood over a twenty-year period. There is a vast collection of correspondence, both personal and professional. Since 1963, I kept every letter I ever received from my agent, various editors, publishers, movie producers and directors, publicists, and other professionals with whom I've worked, and they are included. I've published a handful of photo essays and all my transparencies and photographs from those projects are a part of the archives going to UNM. So too all the artwork I've created over the years, including the original drawings (both published and unpublished) from a decade's worth of my political cartoons.

Many years of my novel notes are included. There are file drawers of newspaper reviews of my work, author profiles, and interviews I've given over many years. Also research files for some of the books I've published. All the journals I've kept since age fifteen are included with the archives (subject to restrictions for a certain time). I have included first published editions of everything I've ever published. There are also two four-drawer file cabinets of what I call my "Activities Files," which contain files from every talk I've given, articles written, workshops attended, and political rallies, from 1970 to the present. Also copies of publishing contracts. And by the time the last files are turned over, I will even have included tax records going back to 1958!

My archives are quite vast, very thorough, and pretty well organized: I've spent years getting them in order and doing a pretty complete inventory. You might say it's way Too Much Information. On the other hand, it's a really macroscopic overview of my life and work. And if my work eventually fades away, the archives should still be an interesting historical and social record of the last half of the twentieth century in northern New Mexico.

FRASER: Can you explain the background of the archive's establishment? Were you approached by the university, and if so, what were your initial reactions to the idea of setting up an official collection of your papers?

NICHOLS: Many years ago I began talking with the University of New Mexico about my archives. This was in the late 1980s. I had lost my home in a divorce and wound up storing boxes and boxes of manuscripts and correspondence in a storage locker. A lot of the stuff was fairly helter-skelter. So I started organizing everything into manuscript boxes and manila folders. Since my teenage years, I had kept letters from many friends and girlfriends stashed in trunks. I sorted through them, organized them in files, placed them in alphabetical order, bought more file cabinets. Bit by bit, I arranged scads of material in order and started to realize that I had kept an astonishing record. Once organized, the archives seemed interesting not just on a personal level, but also as a social and historical record. Certainly, it was a very comprehensive record of a writer's creative process.

Anyway, over the years UNM and I talked. For ages, I didn't want to unload the archives because I used them in research for all my books, and I dreaded cutting myself off from these creative roots, so to speak. But at 68, I finally relented because, frankly, I wanted to pass on the material before I croaked. I mean, I could not imagine my kids, the day after I expire, standing in front of all the file cabinets and bookshelves of manuscript boxes saying, "What the hell do we do now?"

FRASER: Do you have any qualms about the archive? Are you at all nervous about the potentially sensitive nature of some of the personal material in the collection?

NICHOLS: Of course I have qualms. First: I'm terrified that the moment the archives are gone I will decide to write a 4,000-page autobiography about my scintillating and brilliant life . . . but all the evidence will be at UNM 130 miles away from me. Second: Anyone who delves into the manuscripts of books I both did and did not publish will become privy to my huge feet of clay, my infantile dysfunctions, the horrendously puerile and bad novels I've written, and so forth. Third: Yes, the sensitive personal material, mostly diaries and letters, is disconcerting and will have to be restricted for a period of years. I never destroyed anything, on the grounds that censorship is a bane to understanding human behavior. Of course, we all censor ourselves relentlessly. However, one role of an artist is to reveal true human behavior. Art is a way we understand ourselves—the good, the bad, and the ugly. So I did not destroy lots of material that is quite unflattering.

FRASER: What do you see as the value of literary archives in general? As a writer, have you ever availed yourself of the opportunity to study a specific author's papers in a special collection?

NICHOLS: The value of literary archives is the value of any historical material or artifacts. They can be fascinating maps of human endeavor and behavior, and interesting far beyond a specific individual and his or her papers. As a writer and researcher, I have never studied an author's papers in a special collection, but I have read and enjoyed and learned from thousands of books—novels, biographies, history, sociology, diaries, letters—that depended on authors' papers in special collections for their research. Hence I have benefited a lot from special collections.

FRASER: In past interviews, you have noted some of your earliest literary influences: F. Scott Fitzgerald, Ernest Hemingway, Carson McCullers, Damon Runyan. Do these figures still inform and inspire your work, or has their hold on your imagination faded over time? As your career has unfolded, what other writers have contributed to your sense of the craft? Are there screenwriters or memoirists, for instance, who stimulate your production and show you new paths of discovery?

NICHOLS: My earliest influences remain powerful, including Damon Runyon and Hemingway and Carson McCullers. There were hundreds of others who shaped my imagination, my desire, and my "talent" when I was younger. When I got politicized in the 1960s and 1970s, I absorbed a raft of important writers like Malcolm X, George Jackson, Ida Tarbell, and Mother Jones. I was also moved deeply by books like Émile Zola's *Germinal*, Robert Caro's *The Power Broker*, *The Village of Ben Suc* by Jonathan Schell. All my life I have kept soaking up the influences. I used to tell people (in a Will Rogers vein) that "I never met a book I didn't like." My taste pretty much runs everywhere, from *Rally Round the Flag Boys* by Max Schulman, to *Hitler's Willing Executioners* by Daniel Goldhagen. Although I worked on Hollywood screenplays for almost two decades, I never studied screenwriting or screenwriters. These days it's difficult to find people who "stimulate my production." As I get older, I have trouble finding writers who blow me away.

FRASER: Critics have often compared you to John Steinbeck. I wonder why his name doesn't appear on your list of literary influences. Is that simply a casual omission, or are you ambivalent about being associated with him?

NICHOLS: Oh gosh, of *course* John Steinbeck was one of my influences. I read almost everything he ever wrote and I tried to imitate and emulate all of it. I have no ambivalence at being associated with him—I'm flattered. But you must understand that I have no ambivalence at being associated with almost *anybody* I've read. Call me Zelig! There's no way for me to list all the writers that I have loved, studied, wanted to plagiarize. What about Thomas Wolfe,

Katherine Anne Porter, James Baldwin, Beatrix Potter, Truman Capote? I have always been very impressionable, and I think I have tried to soak up *everybody*. You might say I have had no discretion whatsoever. I love Gide, Françoise Sagan, Gabriela Mistral, Miguel Asturias, Garcia Márquez, George Eliot, Denise Chávez . . .

FRASER: So much of your writing attacks the lumpen ineffectiveness of government, and the bulldozing effects of empire and territorial seizure. In *The Magic Journey* you refer to the empowered elite as "plump bastards." You mention Malcolm X and Mother Jones. What additional figures have shaped your social consciousness and spoken to you as fellow chronicles of the impoverished, the exploited, the abused?

NICHOLS: Upton Sinclair, Theodore Dreiser, Lucy Parsons, Piri Thomas, Angela Davis, Toni Morrison, Chellis Glendinning, Demetria Martínez, Elizabeth Gurley Flynn, Tillie Olsen, Meridel Le Sueur, Helen Hunt Jackson, Vine Deloria, Jr., Dee Brown, Leslie Silko, Frantz Fanon, Matthew Josephson, Juan Rulfo, Martín Espada, Víctor Jara, Violeta Parra, Marge Piercy, Eduardo Galeano, Louise Erdrich, Nâzim Hikmet, Paulo Freire, Enriqueta Vasquez, Betita Martínez, Mariano Azuela, Howard Zinn, Hans Koning, Rubén Darío, Alan Sillitoe, José Martí, Che Guevara, Primo Levi, Simone de Beauvoir, García Lorca, Alice Walker, Edwidge Danticat...and that's just for starters. I could go on and on.

FRASER: You are widely known as an ardent environmentalist. In your essay "Keep It Simple," while discussing our often destructive relationship with the natural world, you note, "No matter what, we all do damage. Nevertheless, it's real easy to reduce the damage we do." Our nation now has a new president who appears committed to greener initiatives. What kind of hopes do you have for the Obama administration in terms of the environment, and if you could offer him some educated counsel, what would it be?

NICHOLS: As an "environmentalist," this is what I believe: A climax capitalist society based on profit and growth, such as now runs the world, is incompatible with survival of the biology that sustains us. We must seriously restrict our resource consumption and economic and population expansion, and work toward human justice and a more equitable distribution of wealth. This demands a radical social transformation that doesn't seem in the cards right now. Perhaps the Obama administration can make us signatories of the Kyoto Protocol, protect some endangered species, initiate social programs for the poor and the unemployed. But I do not now see Obama as significantly altering where we are headed or how fast we are going to get there. We need truly radical change. Let's hope this new administration can at least begin.

FRASER: Your grandfather was a curator of fishes at the American Museum of Natural History in New York City. Was he a major force behind your commitments to the natural world?

NICHOLS: My grandfather and namesake, John T. Nichols, was a well-known naturalist and a big influence on me. Way more of an influence was my dad, David G. Nichols, a professional naturalist in his own right. He taught me as a child to love birds, plants, mammals, insects, reptiles—the entire web of life. My dad explained that web, he loved it, and it occupied his entire life. His respect for the natural world certainly helped shape my destiny from an early age.

FRASER: You have described the writing process by analogy to cross-country running, which you did competitively in college. You've stated that both activities are "long and painful." What facets of the writing life lead you to define the craft in these terms?

NICHOLS: Believe me, for yours truly, writing is not half as long and painful as life on the line in an auto factory would have been long and painful, or life as an insurance salesman would have been long and painful. My life has been a breeze. For most of it, I have loved writing. I'm not a very good writer, which means I have to rewrite 100 times, and even then the outcome usually stinks. It's very hard for me to write decently, and when/if I do, I also need a lot of luck. I'm not a natural. I'm very clumsy. I'm sentimental, riddled with clichés, flaws everywhere. Not very grown up. What have I got going for me? Well, I have energy, I try to be full of life, and I have a sense of humor.

FRASER: Can you discuss the similarities and differences inherent in writing novels, memoirs, and screenplays? Have you ever tried your hand in other genres such as poetry?

NICHOLS: Novels can ramble all over the universe; screenplays are mostly short stories. If you think of a novel as an epic poem, like Homer's *Odyssey*, then a screenplay is like a sonnet—very short, fourteen lines every time. If you make a film from a novel you should buy the book, then throw it away. *Then* you write a script, which is a totally different medium. One hundered and ten pages, and most of it is air. Memoirs, I don't know. They are limited because they need to be based on what's factually "true." So you are restricted. Novels offer immense freedom. I've never been able to write poetry or short stories because I've never been very much interested in poetry or short stories.

FRASER: In the *Devil's Dictionary*, Ambrose Bierce wittily defines the novel as "a short story padded." You can be a truly expansive writer: a Nichols novel can run over five hundred pages. What do you like most about the panoramic possibilities of the novel?

NICHOLS: Really, only three of my novels have ever run close to five hundred pages, and those are *Milagro, The*

Magic Journey, and *The Nirvana Blues*. When I wrote those three books, I was in love with the macroscopic overview: Dickens, Tolstoy, Hugo. *A writer must know everything*. But some of my other novels, for example *The Sterile Cuckoo*, are very short, almost novellas. I've always been torn between wanting to write big brawling novels like *Bleak House* and *Moby Dick*, and little, precise, powerful books like *Burning Patience* by Antonio Skármeta, *Night* by Elie Wiesel, and *The Fall* by Albert Camus. If you are good, or just lucky, both kinds of books can say everything.

FRASER: *The Empanada Brotherhood*, your latest book and your eleventh novel, is relatively short. It consists of about sixty thematically interwoven vignettes that rely for their resonances on suggestiveness and evocation. Would you say that you are testing out new strategies of compression in this work?

NICHOLS: The *Empanada Brotherhood* is a story told in many short chapters, but each one develops the plot. The gimmick is that the reader needs to do some work in order to understand the underside of the iceberg that isn't so openly apparent but that is very much in evidence on every page if you just pay attention and are able to put yourself into the shy narrator's shoes. Every novel strives to find its methodology and tone. Another very short novel I've published is *An Elegy for September*. Both *Elegy* and *Empanada* are different from, say, *American Blood*, which is very different from *Milagro*, which is very different from *Conjugal Bliss*, which is very different from *The Voice of the Butterfly*. For me, it's always interesting to work on projects that have unique problems (for me) to solve. That's what makes the writing fun.

FRASER: You once quipped that your writing career has amounted to "one bad book after another." What do you think drives that kind of comic self-deprecation? Is it perhaps a defense mechanism against complacency?

NICHOLS: Look, I really have spent my career writing one bad book after another—no kidding. If you don't believe me, go to the University of New Mexico library and try to wade through the artery-clogging sentiment and hysteria of draft after draft of all the puerile (and thankfully unpublished) novels I have created since I was seventeen years old that now reside in my archives lodged in catacombs below the Center for Southwest Research. I dare you. I'm not being self-deprecating, I'm being truthful. Yes, I have also published nineteen books, all of which have life and energy, but most of them could also use some serious tweaking, rewriting, and editing to make them better. Too late now. It is so much more difficult for me to try and write today than it was when I was twenty, penning those awful books in college. I think it's really important not to take yourself too seriously, and don't get a fat head from, or get discouraged by, your press clippings. Writing is fun. For me it has been a good job. There's nothing mystical about it—it's a lot of work like most any other job. But nothing I've published could possibly lead to thoughts of complacency. What wishful thinking.

FRASER: You published your first novel, *The Sterile Cuckoo*, at the age of twenty-four. What do you regard as some of your earliest strengths as a writer, and how do you see these qualities sustaining themselves during your lengthy career?

NICHOLS: My early strengths were that I had effusive energy and desire and a willingness to work very hard, listen to criticism, and keep knocking my head against the wall. I was a pro at taking rejection. I had the ability to keep trying until perhaps I staggered into a solution. My brain wasn't disciplined but my work habits were. These work habits have sustained themselves for over forty-five years. I just got up every morning and packed a sandwich in my little black lunch box and headed off to the steel mill, six days a week, fifty weeks a year, for the last forty-five years. I can say, "I was a writer," and feel proud that at least I put in the work and the time. I tried.

FRASER: How about your earliest challenges? Were there particular obstacles that you struggled to overcome, fissures that you sought to close? How successful do you think you've been in addressing your challenges while seeking to break new artistic ground?

NICHOLS: My earliest challenge was simply trying to write a coherent, publishable book. *The Sterile Cuckoo* was about the eighth novel I had written. Shortly after publishing my first two novels, my biggest obstacle became my radical politics, forged during the Vietnam War. At first, I could not understand how to mix politics and art, how to overcome, or how to incorporate in my work, my own rabid polemics. I got lucky with *The Milagro Beanfield War*, and managed to realize a political vision with the following two novels in the New Mexico Trilogy, *The Magic Journey* (my favorite), and *The Nirvana Blues*. Since then, I doubt I've broken any new artistic ground. I've published some environmental screeds and a few fairly gentle memoirs, and an odd range of novels from *American Blood* to *The Voice of the Butterfly*. They run a gamut and I like their diversity. My latest novel, *The Empanada Brotherhood*, was a long exercise in striving to write a really quiet and simple book, the opposite of my often manic tendencies. I attempted to leave the real story unsaid and yet completely evident. It was a fascinating struggle for me to try and pare down the writing to those bare bones. I'm disappointed when critics say, "Nothing happens in *The Empanada Brotherhood*." My god, there is *so much happening underneath*.

FRASER: As a film, *The Milagro Beanfield War* won a relatively wide audience and received an award from the Political Film Society. Yet in your essay "Night of the Living Beanfield," you offer a jaundiced view of the project, calling it a "traumatic experience." Do you still feel the same way?

NICHOLS: *Milagro* received an award from The Political Film Society? Who are they? Well, first of all, making any movie is going to be a traumatic experience for everyone involved. That's the nature of the beast. Everything always goes wrong: all the creative people are temperamental idiots, and the producers are like slime-ball Chicago gangsters or crazy Wall Street hedge-fund managers trying to keep the film on budget, the cocaine and heroin off the set, and the director from having a nervous breakdown. You could read John Gregory Dunne or Larry McMurtry or William Goldman on making movies and get a lot of laughs and a lot of shrieks. Working with Hollywood is frustrating, weird, interesting, traumatic, funny, and well-rewarded financially. There's lots of stress and lots of hilarious stories about disasters, near disasters, and totally goofy tragedies and halleluiahs. The making of *Milagro* was especially disorganized, and especially difficult for me because Redford's presence in a northern New Mexico location blew the project all out of proportion, and I took a lot of flak from my friends and political buddies and the local publicity juggernaut. My fifteen minutes of fame were a bit psycho. Maybe it was like winning the lottery and suddenly everybody wants your millions. I didn't have the millions, just the publicity hype. I was very glad when it was over. "Night of the Living Beanfield" is simply a shtick I wrote about it—to get some laughs.

FRASER: You refer to *The Magic Journey* as your favorite among the books you've written. What makes it stand out in your mind? The book is partially set in the 1930s. It must have required months of historical research.

NICHOLS: I put everything including the kitchen sink into *The Magic Journey*, everything I believe in, and all the energy and skill I could muster to make it work and be powerful. The book is not as much fun to read as *Milagro*, but I think it has more soul and a much tougher and more realistic political message. The book actually covers from 1930 to 1970. And, yes, I did a lot of research, but a majority of the research was geared toward understanding the town of Chamisaville at what was then the current day, the early 1970s. In essence, I always thought of *Magic Journey* as a contemporary novel that just had a rather long introduction. April Delaney comes home in 1970 on page 197 with still 332 pages to go during her life in present-day Chamisaville. The book was eventually published in 1978.

FRASER: Novalis, the early German Romantic, wrote that "Philosophy is really homesickness—it is the urge to be at home everywhere." Your novels seem to capture a similar longing, a quest among your principal characters to discover places (and psychological spaces) where they can feel rooted and safe. Yet for some reason, your characters perennially reside "betwixt Here and There," to quote from *The Magic Journey*. They never seem to reach final destinations or comfortable homes. What do you think motivates this tendency in your writing?

NICHOLS: After my first two novels, every book I've written, except for the last one, is set in my home territory of northern New Mexico. Some of the books rail against the destruction of that home, others laud it to pieces. Different stories with different plots are told, but they all take place in the same place—my home where I do feel rooted but never safe, because "safe" is pretty much an illusion for all of us. Most of us don't reach a final destination until we die. As for comfortable homes? Who do you know who truly lives in a comfortable home, be it actual, philosophical, psychological? That's not really the human condition, is it?

FRASER: You have collaborated with major film directors and actors such as Alan Pakula and Robert Redford. What do writers learn from working on screenplays and movie sets? Faulkner and Fitzgerald both earned income from stints in Hollywood—though not without some injury to their personal lives. Is it dangerous or compromising for a serious writer to work for the film industry, or is that merely a myth?

NICHOLS: Over the years, I also worked on three films with Constantin Costa-Gavras, one film each with Karel

Reisz and Louis Malle, a couple of movies with Ridley Scott, another with producers Bill Panzer and Peter Davis, and I wrote a TV mini-series for CBS that never got off the ground. I earned a decent salary and I enjoyed my adventures in the screen trade. What I learned from working on films is that screenplays are short stories, very compact and complex Chinese puzzles, and immensely difficult to construct well.

I never hung out on sets. Fitzgerald and Faulkner screwed up their personal lives because they were hopeless drunks wherever they lived and during whatever they were working on. Nobody forced them to blow all their dough and go to Hollywood, and Hollywood paid them well. Probably *saved* their lives, in fact. Sure, Hollywood is a rough business, but so is publishing or working in a restaurant or on an assembly line. It's not dangerous or compromising for a serious writer to work for the film industry any more than it's dangerous and compromising for a serious writer to teach at Cornell, or bag groceries at Smith's, or work for an insurance company, or harvest potatoes in the San Luis Valley. We all have to earn a living. And Hollywood offers a better living than most industries for those who can hack it. Serious movies get made, and they are scripted by serious writers. I have little patience with writers who kvetch about losing their integrity while banking all that bread.

FRASER: As a way of ending, I wonder how you would describe the novel, as a literary form, in terms of its value to contemporary culture? In what meaningful ways does it differ from film, for instance, as an instrument of potential social change?

NICHOLS: It's pretty tough to change the world or the culture with a novel. That's a simple fact of limited distribution, which means limited influence. On the other hand, during its first day of release, almost any film (from *Robocop* to *High School Musical*) will be seen by more people than have read the Bible since Gutenberg first invented movable metal type in the fifteenth century. So which medium do you think has more potential for social change?

TESTIMONY FROM AN UNDERWATER ORINTHOLOGIST

BY JACLYN DWYER

Reporter: What would you say to Connie Bostic, if you could?

Janeske Vargas: Not a thing.

Reporter: Do you have anything to say to her family?

Janeske Vargas: No. Why should I?

Reporter: Well, you killed…

Janeske Vargas: They'll get over it. Get over it.

1.

My rapist is going to kill Janeske Vargas. He's been assigned the case, and the DA is asking for the death penalty. Sometimes I think of Janeske Vargas and I want to ask her, "What does it feel like that he has this power over you?" I want to know what it is like for her and to tell her what it has been like for me. But Janeske Vargas is a murderer, and so she's not like me at all. We are nothing alike, but still, I feel connected to her. As if we are sisters in some way.

2.

Sometime during the year that I was with him, my sister was raped by her best friend's older brother. It was only one time, but there were two of them. They hurt her in ways that weren't sexual. She has always been feistier than me, more determined to win. I imagine she fought back hard, and they returned with more violence. I wasn't there to see it or to hold her hand. I try not to think of it much. All she ever said was that one boy held her arms, the other her legs. She was thirteen.

Sometimes, I try to decide which is worse, as if this is a decision that can be made. I can't tell. Most times I think our lives are two parallel versions of the same thing. Two versions of the same self. The same, but different. We are twins born on different days.

What happened to me was not violent, but it happened more than once. It was every day, sometimes twice a day, for nine months. The length of human gestation.

It's not really what you'd think. It's really not such a big deal, the everyday part. It becomes like brushing your teeth, combing the knots out of your hair, shaving your legs. Something you hate to do, but something that has to be done. It becomes unavoidable, a tedious part of a daily routine. You learn to stop praying for God to make it stop, because He won't. You learn to adjust, to pray instead for it to be over quickly. You become an adept liar and pray for someone to see through you, but no one does. No one can believe the unbelievable. Sometimes even you cannot believe it, which is why you write it all down. You learn how to give in because it makes it easier for you, makes it hurt less, bleed less. You learn how to clean up the blood and to always pack extra underwear in your school bag before he comes to pick you up. You learn to give up hope because when you get in the car and see that his belt buckle is already undone, it crushes you inside. Instead, you expect it. You feel strange when it doesn't happen. You wonder what is wrong with you.

The first time, when you got to school you went straight to the bathroom, walking with stilt-legs, a funny walk that you tried to mollify, to take care of the blood. You tried to ignore the gossiping girls who were in there applying mascara, while you packed toilet paper like it was gauze. They made their lips slick and shiny with the spongy pink end of a Covergirl wand, lips that had probably never been kissed. Lips like yours. You were grateful that your uniforms compelled you to wear tights. They held the shoddy bandage in place.

See, after it happens the first time, it doesn't really matter whether it's once, twice or two hundred times. You stopped counting after twenty-eight. You lost count and you couldn't find your way back. At first you saw it as a way of keeping track, but eventually the numbers lost their meaning. Numbers would become important again several months later. You would resume counting the days with a heady anxiety. You planned a speech to deliver to your mother, how you were pregnant with the Second Coming, a virgin birth, Immaculate Conception, because you couldn't tell her what had really happened. You were lucky that you never had to give this speech. After sixty-three days, your period finally came.

HEADLINE: Woman Sets Friend on Fire

Janeske Vargas was arrested for starting a deadly fire that killed her best friend on December 13. Vargas, a hairdresser, smiled into television cameras, while police escorted her into the station.

Accoring to Vargas, both she and the victim, Connie Bostic, were drinking vodka at Bostic's home in Skippack when the two began arguing. Vargas had also taken Xanax, an anti-anxiety drug, said the District Attorney, at a news conference yesterday. According to reports the argument began over a cell phone.

Vargas reportedly said, "Connie took my cell phone. She wouldn't give it back, so I hit her on the head with the bottle." Bostic then accused Vargas of being a "bad friend." Vargas reacted, "I just opened the bottle of vodka and poured what was left over her. Then I grabbed the nail polish remover and I dumped that too. I lit her on fire and she just went up in flames."

3.
The first time, he smothered me. "Do you know how easy it would be for me to kill you?" His backyard was a cornfield. The DA lived across the street. I didn't know if this was

a threat or a mere observation. "I could lay your body out there, in the middle of the corn, and nobody would find you for days. Nobody would look for you there. Nobody knows that you're here." I felt like he had already obliterated my existence. There was no way for me to die anymore. I was beyond death.

He held a t-shirt over my face until I passed out. Maybe it was a blanket, a sheet, or an empty pillowcase. Maybe it was only the weight of his body suffocating me. I couldn't breathe. I was gasping for air. I woke up on the bed, groggy, unable to remember how I'd gotten there. I was compelled to fill the gaping hole, but there was nothing. A blank space separated me from my last memory inside that room. I'd been on the floor, his hands wrapped around my wrists, squeezing so hard I thought my bones might break. My ulna and radius would snap together and fuse into a single arm bone. BLANK. I was on the bed, and I didn't care what was happening because I was too concerned about what I had missed. What I couldn't remember happening. Had it been an hour? A few minutes? There was this huge chunk of my life missing that I would never get back. I scolded myself for not being able to stay awake. I worried about pregnancy. I was fourteen.

He'd disseminated my clothes into the corners of the room, so that I had to scramble to collect them all. He laughed while I crawled. I felt the need to keep my body close to the ground. Standing, at this point, was incomprehensible. I crawled like a baby. I slithered, an animal without functioning limbs. He grabbed me by the shoulder and threw me backward. He crumpled my panties into his fist, a magician making tissue disappear. I went for my shirt, slinking along the adjacent wall. Again he beat me. Leapt on top of me, slammed me into the ground. Then I gave up. I was no fun for him. I sat hugging my knees to my chest. I waited, and eventually he gave back my clothes. He threw them at me, those articles that he'd collected in his hands. When I picked up my shirt, my tin of lip balm fell out of the pocket. He picked it up. He wouldn't give it back. Each time I tried to grab it, he'd pull his hand away, laughing more and more. He pulled me onto his lap and made me dip my finger into the tin and smear it over my lips.

... AND THE SWAN

A sudden blow: the great wings beating still
Above the staggering girl, her thighs caressed
By his dark webs, her nape caught in his bill,
He holds her helpless breast upon his breast.
How can those terrified vague fingers push
The feathered glory from her loosening thighs?

I was late to school a lot. He wrote notes, and sometimes walked me into the office, giving me excuses to slip into my first class five minutes before it ended.

4.

Even though we were born two years apart, we were raised to be twins. If we had been twins, my sister would have weighed more at birth because in utero the aggressive twin steals all the nutrients from the weaker one.

Until adolescence, we shared the same friends, the same activities. We were perfect together. I ate the icing, she ate the cake. She took all the cheese off my pizza, I wiped the sauce off hers with my crust. Even to people outside the family we were a single unit: the girls. People who saw us every day for softball or swimming knew us as a pair and had to ask when they saw only one of us, "Which one are you?"

She was a chatterbox, I was painfully shy. I spoke only when she was around as if she somehow facilitated my speech. Without her I was lost. Mute. We attended the same high school. One year we were roommates in college. Then we commuted together and shared the same car. When I was accepted to the Overseas Program at Oxford University, I actually considered staying at home because I couldn't imagine being apart from her.

SCHWANENGESANG

Swans are named not only for their colors, but for the sounds they make. *The Trumpeter Swan* was a book I read in fourth grade. It sounds like a French horn. The Whooper Swan is a loud honker. The Mute Swan has a voice but chooses not to speak. It has a warning call. A throaty sound escapes from its beak when it is threatened. Otherwise, the only sound of the Mute Swan is the whooshing of its wings as they propel the heavy bird into flight. When it is about to die, the Mute Swan sings a song so beautiful it is painful to hear, but people listen. This is the swan song. A heartbreaking noise. A radiant sound. Something I have never heard but might try to sing myself one day.

5.

That summer, before I left for a year abroad in England, my sister told me about Anton, and I thought this would bring us closer than ever. Instead, it drew us apart.

There were three of them: one Welsh, one Scottish, and one from Liverpool. The Welsh boy was married, though he'd taken off his ring; the Scot was twenty-four with two kids by separate mothers, a fact we were unaware of until he'd taken off his shirt to reveal their faces, which had been tattooed on his chest. The trip, a family vacation of sorts, was planned before I knew I would be going to live in England for a year. My parents were in a different room, down the hall, around the corner. My sister and I had gone out. They offered wine with dinner. There was a bar. She was drinking something blue. I was drinking something red. I didn't like it so my sister drank them both while we hung around the hotel lobby.

The Welsh's wife called his cell phone several times, and he answered it once. My sister had gone back to the room. She'd said she was going to watch the sunrise at four a.m. through an observatory window. I didn't notice her standing on the balcony until the Liverpool boy said, "Hey, I think your sister needs you. She looks worried."

When I turned, I saw her at the top of the stairs. She called down to me, and ushered me toward her with a wave of her hand. She was wearing a zippered sweatshirt, with nothing underneath. "I need you to help me." The Scot was in our room, in her bed apparently. "He won't leave," she said. "Make him leave."

I was disappointed in her. Still, I was the older sister. I was supposed to protect her. When I opened the door to our room, the Scot was reclining on our bed, shirt off, the tattooed faces of his babies staring back at me. A boy over the right chambers of his heart, a daughter by the left.

"OK. It's time for you to go now," I said.

He was slow to leave. I kept pushing him and he kept pressing my sister, begging her to let him stay. "She's only nineteen," I kept saying, which she didn't like. She didn't want me babying her.

She pulled me into the bathroom to whisper, "I can do this myself." She said, "I can handle this." I had no reason not to believe her.

"I'm coming back in five minutes and going to bed. He's gotta be out in five minutes. I'm outside the door, waiting. If he's not out in five minutes I'm coming in."

"OK," she said. The time passed on my watch. I didn't hear anything inside, so I gave her the full five minutes, knocked, and turned my key. She was sitting on the bed, undressed from the waist up. The image of her pre-pubescent-looking breasts pressed itself into my mind. The Scot was naked. The faces of his babies stared at me.

"Out," I screamed at him. "Now. You have to leave. Out!"

When he left, I told her how stupid she was. I was yelling at her. "Is this how you want to lose your virginity?"

"No. I'm drunk. I think I'm drunk," she said.

"What do you mean? Why didn't you say this before? Do you know what could have happened?"

"I know. I don't know," she said. "I'm not really a virgin anyway." It was an afterthought. I could have let it pass, but maybe she said it for a reason, maybe she was inviting me into conversation, one I wasn't sure I wanted to enter.

"What do you mean?" I asked. My sister was sitting on her bed now, and I sat on mine. I wanted to curl under the covers. We had to be up in two hours, but I wanted a deep, deep sleep.

"You have to promise not to tell Mom," she said.

I promised.

"The summer after seventh grade," she began, "I went to her house to play, and she wasn't there." I didn't move while she kept talking, "Her brother, Anton, answered the door, he said she was out shopping with her mom and she'd be home soon. So I went inside to wait. Anton had a friend over."

I immediately thought, *She's lying*. I didn't want to hear anymore. I wanted to scream, "Shut up." But I said nothing. My hands clenched at my sides, fighting my urge to leave the room. I was compelled to grab my sister and hug her as she sat there on the bed, chewing on her fingers, a nervous habit we shared, but I couldn't bear to look at her. So I stared at the wall, trying hard not to hate her.

I said, "I'm tired. I'm going to bed."

I did not share my story with her.

Four months later, while I was at Oxford, Anton crashed his car and died. After a late night he was speeding around a bend and tore through the aluminum barrier. Beyond that was a tree. The car crumpled like tin, and his body was crushed within it.

6.

When I was in England, my sister called me only once during the entire year that I was there.

"Anton died," she said.

"What? How?"

"He crashed his car speeding. I can't go to the funeral."

"I know you can't. All those people crying over him, saying how he was such a great kid. You can't hear that."

"Mom keeps telling me I have to go. 'She was your best friend. You have to go.' It's only because she's going and she won't know what to say when they ask her where I am."

My sister had suddenly, mysteriously, stopped talking to Anton's sister the summer she was thirteen, even though she lived down the street. The only girl my sister's age in our development. In eighth grade my sister made new friends my mother didn't like. Girls who cut on their arms and legs with Exacto knives, who wore black lipstick and chanted "I am whore. Hear me roar." One girl wrote a note to my sister: *Just make sure that if you kill yourself, you do it right, because if you don't, they'll lock you up. Just look at Robyn.*

Robyn had been hospitalized on three separate occasions: a failed hanging, a failed overdose, and an accidental cut that went too deep.

And so, in ninth grade, my parents sent my sister to a Catholic school, just as they had done with me.

"Let me talk to Mom."

"No no no, I'll figure it out."

"Last night some guy tied me to the bed with his head scarf."

"What?"

"I thought it'd make you feel better. It kind of freaked me out."

"I have to go," she said.

Aesop: The swan, who had been caught by mistake instead of the goose, began to sing as a prelude to its own demise. His voice was recognized and the song saved his life.

7.

I was drunk. The party was across the hall but our apartment door was open. Our kitchen was the bar I had been tending earlier that night. Our bedrooms didn't lock. There was a pirate at the party who followed me into my room when I left to go to bed.

He told me that homosexuality was a bigger sin than rape because at least rape was in the Bible. I laughed. He told me that he could do anything he wanted because he'd joined the crew team and was working out. He asked if I wanted him to display his strength. I told him to get out. He wouldn't leave. He came closer. "There's no use screaming," he said. "No one can hear you."

The pirate pulled off the scarf that had wrapped his head all night and pushed me backward onto the bed. He held my right hand against the headboard while I tried to pull away and hit him with my left. My flatmate must have heard me screaming. He flushed the toilet outside my bedroom. The rush of water startled the pirate enough for him to pause and realize what he was doing. He stood up, apologizing profusely, while I untied myself and screamed at him to leave. The pirate forgot his scarf and his mobile phone, which I found the following morning when it rang and woke me up.

I didn't tell my flatmates what had happened, even when they asked. No one ever spoke of any of this again, until my sister came to visit me that spring.

"Let's go to Christchurch where *Harry Potter* was filmed. We can pet the horses in Port Meadow, see the pub where Tolkien wrote *Lord of the Rings.*"

"This is my vacation," she said "I want to relax."

I dragged her around town. She kept complaining that she was tired, jet-lagged. She took a four-hour nap that afternoon while I wrote a paper on *Ulysses.* That night, she stayed up after I went to bed. She took pictures of my friends in their beds, surprised them by opening their bedroom doors. The light flashed in their eyes. Some of them couldn't get back to sleep, so they came out to entertain her. She complained that I had abandoned her for sleep. She told them all about the pirate who had tied me to the bed.

HEADLINE: Vargas Escapes Death

Yesterday in court, Janeske Vargas showed no sympathy and no remorse when she admitted to one count each, arson and homicide. Vargas confessed that she intentionally set a fatal fire at Connie Bostic's home. According to police, the victim, Connie Bostic, was so badly burned that they had to use dental records to identify her. Vargas accepted a plea to life in prison in order to avoid the death penalty.

Socrates (just before his execution): You think I cannot see as far ahead as a swan. You know that when swans feel the approach of death they sing, and they sing sweeter and louder on the last days of their lives because they are going back to that God whom they serve.

8.

The last time it happened was in public. My mother saw.

We were at a swim meet, so I was half naked already. He asked me to come to the parking lot to see his new car. He said he wanted to take me for a short drive.

"I have to swim soon. I don't want to miss my race."

If I went with him, I didn't think I'd come back alive. This was his last shot with me. He was moving away. He was so desperate that day, shaking, unable to control himself. And all of this in public, when he'd been so careful to cover things up before. He was scaring me.

He picked me up, I wriggled and kicked and he dropped me on the pavement. I tried to crawl away. The pavement dug into my palms, his hands encircled my waist as he lifted me again and tried to stuff me into the car. I held onto the roof, locked my elbows, looked and saw my mother walking toward the entrance, across the parking lot. She stopped mid-stride when our eyes met and she recognized that it was me. "My mother's watching you," I said.

He let go, smiled, and waved to her. Then he elbowed me. "Wave and smile," he said, and I did. My mother walked away. I turned, and rested my back on the window. The glass felt cool against my skin. It was chilly that morning in August. He spun me sideways, one hand around my knees, the other cinching my arms to my side. He began to shove me headfirst into the car, like the Grinch stuffing a too-big package up the chimney. I fell. He dropped me and I fell, and then I ran away.

"Come back," he said. He said he wanted to take me for a drive, to the park nearby. I knew that if I went with him, into those trees, I would never come back.

When I fled, he came after me. He snatched my towel. I went to grab it from him, and he tossed it onto the front seat of the car, like I was a dog dumb enough to play a game of fetch. I began to walk away, and he threw it at me, angrily shouting, calling me names. Baby. He called me a baby all the time. The towel hit me in the back, fell to the macadam. I picked it up and wrapped it around my waist just as three women, mothers of other swimmers on the team, were hurrying out to me.

"Are you all right?"

"I'm fine," I said.

Days later, my mother asked me, "What were you doing with him?"

"Nothing," I said.

That was all we ever said about it. I think she was afraid, like she didn't want to know. I like to think she'd sent those women out for me because she couldn't come herself.

9.

Sometimes, I'm still afraid that someone will find out, that one day when I come across his name in the papers, mine will be printed too, and everyone will know.

NOCTURNE WITH WHAT FOLLOWS

BY KEITH MONTESANO

At two in the morning, there's the constant ominous breath
   of the turbine air conditioner on the North Shepherd

     apartment complex, on that roof where I've watched

couples make love, just to say they're at the highest point
   beneath glowing stars in Richmond: where bruised swirls

     flicker from cop cars, pre-coital drunks flank sidewalks

and lean wavering on side street cars, a friend holding up
   another, pulling hair back so evidence from the night no longer

     stains her clothes. But at 2:06 there's a scream: a woman

or a little girl, crescendo on everyone's mind
   in their dreams. *Call and stay in the house*, is what I hear,

     muffled before the screen door slams on their porch,

the corner house across our street, just footsteps and giant
   shadows. I try to think like a witness, but time here

     doesn't matter now. *What did it sound like?* A gloved hand

wrapped in latex over a mouth? Or something beautiful:
   string quartet hours before at a local wine bar, the slow

     concentrated drunkenness fusing with dusk?

But it's all speculation, and that time has passed. I could say
   it's twenty after when I hear the sirens, could ask why

a little girl was out that late. But that continuous

shrill of summer's breath, eclipsing everything now,
drowns out all the voices: every witness and headline,

everyone passing by to catch a glimpse.

MEETING THE NIGHT SKY

BY PAUL BOGARD

I am neither a scientist nor an astronomer, but I have long been drawn to the night sky. My first memory of the stars is of standing on a northern Minnesota dock with my father when I was five, watching sugary spreads of stars for the slow straight lines of satellites. Still, I lived my first thirty years without knowing this sky—its names, numbers, or secret lives—finally beginning the night I found myself with my college alumni group gathered in the foothills east of Albuquerque.

The city was a spill of butterscotch lights within the Rio Grande valley's slopes. Beyond those slopes swelled volcanoes, behind them Mt. Taylor, and behind that the bald horizon, where russet desert floor met a watercolor sky. The highways hummed with people returning home, people not joining us and Joel, a local astronomer kind enough to brave the chilled desert night.

"So, a good way to get a feel for the curve of the earth," he said, "is to tilt your head and view the horizon."

Twenty heads did as he suggested.

This trick immediately reminds you that you are on a planet, a round rock suspended in space. Do this and you wonder if those who doubted Columbus ever got off the couch. The earth clearly curved beneath the faded strokes of dusky peach, lavender, and rose. I looked to the horizon and felt the earth rolling from the sun, revolving into night.

We began walking down a rutted dirt road after that, toward the canyon campfire where we would spend the next few hours. But I am going to jump ahead here, because thinking of the campfire reminds me of Joel's request of us each later to "tell a story," a story preferably about constellations, myths, or other things celestial. I am jumping ahead, because when we got to me I had no stories to tell.

It's not as though anyone cared, but I let myself down—I realized how little I knew. In fact, here is what I did know: that planets don't twinkle and therefore I could supposedly tell them from stars, and two prominent constellations, the Big Dipper (which actually is technically only part of a constellation) and Orion. That's it. If the night sky were an alphabet, I knew less than a letter.

These days I know more. I watch the night sky knowing that astronomers divide it into eighty-eight sections, each section represented by a constellation, so that any star can be said to be "in" a certain constellation.

And I know more about the constellations, these characters that puzzle the best of us with their amorphous shapes and illogical identities. Two things I try to remember. First, pollution—light and air—has dramatically decreased the luminosity of the night sky, especially for Americans and Europeans, the majority of whom live in cities and suburbs. See the sky in what must resemble its former glory—the numbers, colors, and vividness of the stars—and you realize that a few thousand years ago the Greeks had far more to work with than we do today.

Secondly, most constellations—especially in the northern hemisphere—are Greek figures with which most of us are unfamiliar. I mean, in winter I can see the shape of Auriga, above Orion, with its bright star Capella, but I can't say the first thing that comes to mind is a "charioteer." And that is one of the easy constellations; try identifying Monceros the Unicorn or Cetus the Sea Monster (sounding to me like characters from a kid's book), which both lie near Orion as well. I have found that with an image in mind (a good astronomy book helps), many of the ancient figures (Cassiopeia, Cepheus, Perseus) take shape. Still, I fear some (Ophiuches, the Serpent Holder—I can't even say it, let alone see it) are destined never to register.

When I think of how pollution keeps us from the stars, I think of Henry David Thoreau wondering in 1856, "Is it not a maimed and imperfect nature that I am conversant with?" He was talking about the woods around Walden Pond and how the "nobler" animals such as wolf and moose had been killed or scared away. "I hear that it is but an imperfect copy that I possess," he wrote, "that my ancestors have torn out many of the first leaves and grandest passages, and mutilated it in many places. I should not like to think that some demigod had come before me and picked out some of the best of the stars." Only some 150 years later, this is exactly what our pollution has done. "I wish to know an entire heaven and an entire earth," Thoreau concluded. Me too.

Down near the campfire's warmth, Joel pointed a telescope toward the moon. The telescope resembled a large red gourd, with an eyepiece on the gourd's narrow neck taking the seated viewer closer to the stars.

I wasn't prepared for what I saw that night: the gray-white moon in a sea of black, its surface in crisp relief, brighter than ever before. And the scene's absolute silence. With my naked eye, on nights when the moon climbs slowly, sometimes so dusted with rust and rose, brown and gold tones that it nearly drips dirt colors and seems intimately braided with Earth, it feels close, part of this world, a friend. But through the telescope the moon seemed—ironically—farther away. It was clearer, yes, brilliantly so, but this moon seemed cold, antiseptic—alone in the unfathomable expanse of space.

Many astronomers would just as soon have the moon stay away. They have long since learned about it what they want to know, and its return each month to reflect the sun's brilliance blocks much of the sky from their view.

But I like it when the moon comes back. I want to know all about it, for the same reason I want to know stories about the night sky—to know the world in which I live. I want its names, awareness of its gifts. I want to feel connected to those who lived in this place before me and those who have yet to come. I want to feel connected to where I am.

"Here." Joel offered binoculars. "Take a look through these. Check out the Pleiades, especially." He pointed toward Orion.

Without binoculars the Pleiades were a smudge of six or seven stars. But through the glasses this group transformed into a cushion stuffed with pins of white-point light. "Amazing," I whispered.

"Yeah," he said, "I love the Pleiades."

"Love" isn't a word that astronomers or writers are supposed to use, because "love" is neither objective nor descriptive. But watching a dark night sky, love is often my initial reaction. I think this reaction is instinctual, a human response to the beauty of the world, a response that helps keep our soul alive.

With a clear dark sky I am not so pressed to the concrete by the worries of the day, the pressures of life. The bad news can seem unending, the stories of nature's destruction coming one after another. And then, I step out into the night.

I wish I could go back to when Joel asked, "Paul, can you tell us a story about the stars?" A story? I might have talked about how most people think stars are only white. In fact, some stars are white, but others are shades of red, orange, yellow, or blue. Temperature—which corresponds to the star's age—determines color. Humans struggle to notice these different colors because our eyes work with two kinds of light receptors: rods and cones. The cones are the color sensors, but they don't respond to faint illumination. The rods are more finely attuned to dim light, but they don't discriminate colors. When we look at stars, the sensitive but color-blind rods do most of the work, and so the stars appear mostly white. In a sky deafened by light pollution's blather, the idea that the stars are different colors seems wildly impossible, like something from Willy Wonka or Lewis Carroll. But sit long enough somewhere stars stand in clear three-dimensional beauty and you will see the colors of the rainbow.

I could at least have told of the most beautiful night sky I have seen, when I was eighteen and backpacking in Morocco. How I stumbled from the youth hostel into a snowstorm of stars—a sight so different from the skies in the rest of my life that I wonder sometimes if it was a dream.

Or I could have told of how each star is a sun like ours, just in varying stages of life and at varying distances from us. That's how big the sky is, that every star is a sun and yet only one lights the lake's sand at my feet. All the others are too far away—most so far away that we can't even see them. And without night—if our planet did not rotate away from our own star—we would never see the other suns at all.

What about the Milky Way, a ribbon of distant suns so numerous they cloud the sky? How some ancient cultures, because night was so dark and the Milky Way so light, created constellations from the black gaps in the Milky Way. Or how millions and millions and millions of people today have never been away from city lights to see its beauty.

In his book *The Soul of the Night*, Chet Raymo writes of our galaxy, the Milky Way galaxy, "Our sun is one star in a disk-shaped swarm of several hundred billion stars." And continues,

> I have often constructed a model of the Milky Way Galaxy on a classroom floor by pouring a box of salt into a pinwheel pattern. The demonstration is impressive, but the scale is wrong. If a grain of salt were to accurately represent a typical star, then the separate grains should be thousands of feet apart; a numerically and dimensionally precise model of the Galaxy would require 10,000 boxes of salt scattered in a flat circle larger than the cross-section of the Earth.

This means that every star in our night sky is part of our galaxy. And innumerable galaxies exist outside our galaxy. Space is big. Our night sky is but one tiny plot in a garden too big to imagine.

The distances and numbers bend my brain beyond its reach, as I try to comprehend the incomprehensible. But there also is a regularity in celestial events that thrills me. In 1986, for example, when Haley's comet last passed through, I saw it, newly in my twenties, and when it returns on its seventy-six year cycle, I will be ninety-six—a number as unfathomable as any in the night sky. How will my life have changed between the bookends of Haley's visit? From twenty to ninety-six is the passing of a man's long life. I wonder if it will find me on its return or if it will search in vain, then swing back into space for another seventy-six years to return when my great-grandson has lived his life nearly to its end.

Beautiful by itself, with its clusters and colors and constellations, its showers of blazing rock, the night sky awes me. But most of all, its vastness and beauty makes Earth's beauty more incredible. If we indeed are just one speck of dust in the city of the universe, if the numbers and distances of the night sky are so large that they become nearly meaningless, then let us find the meaning under our feet. There is no other place to go, the night sky makes this clear.

"There's a quote from Ralph Waldo Emerson that I want to leave with you," said Joel, our evening with him concluding. "In 1836, Emerson wrote, 'If the stars should appear one night in a thousand years, how would men believe and adore, and preserve for many generations the remembrance of the city of God which had been shown! But every night come out these envoys of beauty, and light the universe with their admonishing smile.'"

Joel looked around, campfire crackles and the murmur of children in the group the only sounds. "I like that quote just to remember how special it is to see this tonight."

Me too. Because while in the nineteenth century night sky over Concord, Massachusetts, the stars would have stood out in a way that most modern Americans have never seen, and it's easy to wish our sky was still that way, this New Mexico night reminds me:

The beauty we still know is worth preserving. The night sky we still have is worth fighting for. The stars we can see are still there and thousands more (countless more with a telescope) are waiting. To meet and know the night sky is to join the human family, generations upon generations who have gone before us, walking into darkness, imagining what their lives might turn out to be.

GRUMBELINA'S TOMATOES

BY MELISSA OLSON-PETRIE

The official name of the common tomato, *Lycopersicon esculentum*, means "succulent wolf peach," and probably dates from some of the early misapprehensions concerning it.

—Barbara G. Walker,
The Woman's Dictionary of Symbols and Sacred Objects

Grumbelina, the Tomato Woman, or *la Mujer de Tomate*, for that's what we called her, was notorious for two things. She grew the oblong, yellow tomatoes that no one else in the neighborhood could grow. They barely resembled tomatoes, but their taste was beyond divine. The secret was in the skin, she claimed. The tough skins condensed all the flavor of the biggest, ripest beefsteaks into odd, squiggly fruits the size of newborns' fists.

My second tomato was the best. I was seventeen that November, and growing impatient with our town's touristy Día de los Muertos preparations, when Grumbelina ordered me to put one of her tomatoes in my mouth whole. I didn't tell her that I had tried one years ago and couldn't understand what the big deal was. The boys in the club had made me steal some for them and one for me as part of my initiation.

"Elena, eat this," she said. "You're old enough now." She thrust the fruit, which looked more like a jaundiced egg, over the chain-link gate. She pinched it between her thumb and forefinger.

I took it, careful not to graze her crosshatched skin. The tomato was covered with grit, the kind kicked up by fat monsoon raindrops, and it almost slipped out of my hand. I started to wipe it clean, reaching for the short hem of the maternity dress I had made out of my boyfriend's old bluejeans.

"Just eat the tomato." She spoke louder.

I started to bite off the bottom half.

"No, like this." She popped one in her mouth, dirt and all, and grinned while she chewed. The gesture stretched her wrinkly eyes sideways, almost closing them, and broadened her plump cheeks into a full, brown moon with an apron of skin jiggling beneath it.

I couldn't contradict her. Grumbelina's violent overreactions to disappointments of any sort, no matter how minor, were as notorious as her tomatoes. If I didn't do it her way, I imagined she would scream and pelt me with dirt clods as I ran down the road, like she did when the mailman tried to pass her house without so much as delivering another family's junk mail to her.

Biting down slowly, I waited for the tomato to be sour like the one I had tasted seven years before. The boys, after they had realized how nasty the greenish tomatoes were, tried to force me to eat all of them. I fought them off and left, declaring that boys were stupid. However, Grumbelina was too menacing to deny.

Once in my mouth, this tomato wouldn't budge. I bit down harder and harder, grimacing to brace myself for the punishment. Suddenly, I couldn't hear a thing. I could barely keep my mouth shut. Seeds squirted through the gap in my front teeth and against my lips. It reminded me of my boyfriend coming in my mouth, only this tasted so much better. I chewed slowly, knowing I was experiencing what Grumbelina's *abuelita* friends raved about—the perfect tomato. I tried not to swallow too soon, drawing out the moment and realizing that I might not have another chance. Grumbelina could be so stingy with the tomatoes she sold at the South Mountain farmer's market. I wanted to laugh aloud, but I didn't want to lose any of the succulent juice. I closed my eyes to block out Grumbelina's sphinxlike stare of satisfaction. I worried that she could hear my thoughts and knew what I had stolen from her years earlier. Did my reaction give anything away? Now I understood how tomatoes picked by Grumbelina could be so valuable outside Calle Guadalupe. Only she could choose the tomatoes whose taste was as golden as their skin.

I felt I had to say something. It was so important that I say the right thing, but all I could do was nod my head.

Grumbelina seemed to like that. Opening the gate, she told me that I would accompany her to Paramo's Herbaria. It didn't matter that I was headed in the opposite direction, to bring my boyfriend and his tips home from the carwash where I used to work. Grumbelina said she would need a quarter to check her blood pressure at the machine. I had already taken from her, so she took the coin from me. I held it out, pocket lint and all, between my thumb and forefinger. She clasped my wrist, and the quarter dropped into the dust. I bent from my knees to pick it up sideways.

"You carry your baby straight out front, like your mother," she said.

"At Wal-Mart, they follow me around as if I've stuffed one of their precious basketballs up my skirt." I sensed the approach of a lecture about the mother who I no longer lived with, so I jabbed the quarter into Grumbelina's palm and started walking.

Grumbelina's small body was round, like a cherry tomato, and her cadence revealed what a burden it was to carry. We seemed to move slower than possible. Lobo, her adolescent wolf-hybrid, followed us in stages—trot, lay down, wait, trot, lay down. My hipbones clunked in their sockets at the end of each drawn-out step. I began walking rings around Grumbelina, clockwise and then counter, to stop the bone-grinding noises that had started to hurt.

"Why do you grow those yellow tomatoes?" I asked, on my third pass. I looked back at the rows of caged plants surrounding her house. The vines produced fruit earlier, later, and more bountifully than anyone else's. Getting them to bear through 100-degree days, not to mention our months without rain, were some of Grumbelina's secrets.

Late last winter, the sheriff's department raided Grumbelina's home. Deputies burst through the front and back doors suspecting that all the grow lights inside fostered a jungle of marijuana and drug dealers. They found only a sleepy old woman and her tomatoes. If they had staked out a wrong address or if they had spied on a slightly richer neighborhood with their infrared scopes, they might have had better odds on discovering the contraband they sought. But from the helicopter, Grumbelina's had shed the most heat at night—a telltale sign of criminal activity.

As it was, they had someone to arrest but no illegal substances to impound. The deputies were uprooting some seedlings to take back to the crime lab, just in case, when Grumbelina came at them with a spray bottle of her homemade whitefly killer. She squirted one cop's back as he was stuffing her babies into a plastic evidence bag. When he turned around, she hit him with a heavy stream right in the mustache.

"Just a little tobacco, Lux, and beer," she taunted.

He doubled over sputtering and gagging. He retched near the toes of Grumbelina's extra-large tapestry slippers.

A second cop, a woman, was smarter. She threatened Grumbelina with a pepper spray canister that could outdistance the insecticide in both range and effect. She handcuffed Grumbelina and locked her in the awaiting paddy wagon. The cops had been expecting to transport many more. Nonetheless, Grumbelina's dark spirits seemed to fill the van to capacity.

More and more neighbors gathered, attracted by the flashing lights and Grumbelina's owl-like screeches. I watched her through the grille of the paddy wagon's window while the deputies retreated to their cars. Men yelled that the officers were pussies for arresting an old *abuelita*, our *Mujer de Tomate*. The boys started shadowing the cops, getting as close behind them as they could and then running away when the cops whirled around. For once, I was proud of their club.

Even the women came out and stood in the cold with the children. Front and back, people blocked the deputies from driving away with Grumbelina. The officers talked into their radios and scurried around like hens. The deputy who Grumbelina had wounded paced near the EMT truck, swishing and spitting bottled water. Then one cop, a sergeant, stepped forward and tried to tell us to break it up.

"*No habla inglés,*" a cholo shouted.

The sergeant spoke slower.

My oldest brother translated his words into Spanish from across the street, "*Dice que se hace la paja,*" meaning "He says he masturbates often." The neighbor men laughed quietly.

"*No hab-la in-GLES!*" another club member shouted syllable by syllable.

"Damn, Lisa," one cop said. "Why'd you have to arrest her? You wanna start a riot?"

The sergeant signaled the paddy wagon driver, who unlocked the door for Grumbelina.

"She's going to get somebody killed someday," the cop added. I couldn't tell if he was talking about Grumbelina or that woman deputy.

"Oh, you'd rather be taking it in the face with bug spray," Deputy Lisa retorted. Grumbelina walked over and presented her handcuffed wrists to Lisa, who said, "I'm citing you for disorderly conduct. Should be assault."

Grumbelina responded with a predatory look, her mouth tight. In the street lamp, I could see her great white underpants and saggy breasts through her cotton housecoat. She must have been freezing.

"Come over here, baby. I'll protect you," a cholo said motioning toward the woman officer's ass.

"*¡Ya basta!*" Grumbelina yelled at him.

"What did she say? Bastard?" one of the deputies asked.

"She said 'enough already,'" I translated.

Grumbelina, with a rigid back and her fists flattened against her thighs, stalked over to the officer who had the evidence. She scowled at him, silently demanding her plants. He hardly looked at her before opening the trunk of his patrol car and tossing the evidence bag of seedlings at her feet.

"*No respeta nada.*" She cursed his lack of respect. "*¡Tomates por mi raza!*" she said to us, her people, shaking the bag above her head.

The few, mostly women, who knew how good Grumbelina's tomatoes could be, yeahed. Others, like me and the boys from the club, cocked our heads and shrugged. Grumbelina went inside and started warming, replanting, and fertilizing, a hopeless job that would take her until dawn. The neighbors disappeared as fast as they had formed—reabsorbed into adobe shacks and trailers. Only a few club members leaned on cars and fence posts to watch the deputies leave.

I had checked the ground for any of Grumbelina's precious seedlings before going home with my boyfriend. Not a trace. As we moved down the street, I saw my mother who, for once, had something in her arms besides a baby. She carried a mewling puppy, Lobo, onto Grumbelina's front porch and knocked.

"They're called *d'Or*. Organic gold," Grumbelina finally answered my question about why those tomatoes. I could barely hear her over the roar of traffic beyond the I-10 sound wall. When I frowned, she spoke through gritted teeth. "*Dinero. Moneda.* Cash." We were now catty-corner from Paramo's Herbaria, which was newly decorated with plastic *papel picado* cut-outs from China and laughing papier-maché skeletons, including the embarrassing hat woman who held a cigarette and a drink.

"Who's that with Paramo?" Grumbelina asked, squinting across the intersection where flashing yellow and red lights mostly directed cut-through drivers headed to their stucco condos and McMansions on the South Mountain side of the freeway.

"Looks like my Tía Beatriz."

"Does she still grow those roses?"

"She won a ribbon at the fair."

"Ah." Grumbelina nodded her head.

When we walked in the store, Beatriz was examining the source of the blood striping her palm. She licked at it, while the herb vendor scurried around for a bandage. When he saw Grumbelina, he stepped into the back room to put on a clean, white smock.

"You can only use so many of those roses," Grumbelina started. "That's why I like tomatoes. You can smell them on a warm day and dig your teeth into their flesh. They don't nip your fingers either. True, Beatriz? When I die, make sure they cover my grave with tomato plants. Paramo, you are a witness. None of those roses you can smell, but not eat."

"When I die, my roses will weep," Beatriz countered. "They will not bear their hips for anyone but me. Isn't that right, Paramo?" Rose hips were piled on Paramo's scale, next to bouquets of paper marigolds and a pyramid stack of iced sugar skulls, their eyes winking silver foil and their teeth gleaming gold.

Grumbelina sat down at the blood pressure machine wedged between the cash register and a video game. She put her arm in the black, inflatable cuff.

"Paramo, here. The quarter," she said, holding it up.

He nearly fumbled my coin onto the floor before getting it in the slot. The machine hummed as the cuff inflated. Grumbelina set her mouth against the pressure—190 over 122.

"That's nothing," Beatriz said. "Mine is 300, at least. I bet it's higher now. Move over. Elena, dig a quarter from my change purse."

"You've got a leak," Grumbelina said, pointing at Beatriz's bloody hand. "Can't beat me."

"Move." Beatriz used her bony hip to bump Grumbelina's shoulder. "Or are you afraid?"

"I've been working on my blood pressure since I was a *nena*. There's no beating me. I'm even constipated today. Paramo, do you have any rhubarb?"

I handed Beatriz her quarter as she took Grumbelina's seat.

"Ay," she protested as the machine squeezed her skinny arm. She got a puzzling 37 over 000. "This machine, it is broken, no?"

The five-thirty bus had stopped outside. The patio filled with day laborers in baseball caps and low-slung Wranglers. To warm up for the Día de los Muertos festival, someone bought a suitcase of Coors at the stand next-door and passed it around. Two boys in baggy black pants and oversize white T-shirts, who couldn't score beers, came inside the Herbaria looking for ice cream sandwiches.

"Boys, watch this," Grumbelina said, again sitting at the blood pressure machine. She pulled a quarter out of her own pocket. The machine blew up and down, giving her a reading of 158 over 97. Diagnosis: "Hypertension, consult your physician" scrolled by in digital red letters. She seemed disappointed.

"You cheated," Beatriz said. "Move over."

Grumbelina refused, pulling out another quarter. She flexed her wrist back and forth violently and held her hand in a fist so tight that her fingertips glowed white. She grunted at me to put the quarter in the machine. Only this time, when the blood pressure cuff expanded, she yowled as if her arm was caught in a hunter's trap. Lobo ran into the store, skidded across the concrete floor, and finished the howl alongside her. The men from the patio clogged the doorway and pressed their oily faces against the windows trying to get a look. Reading: 206 over 125. Diagnosis: "Stroke alert." She smiled and got up, stumbling and blinking. She grabbed Paramo's counter for support.

"That wolf," Beatriz said. "If he doesn't kill my roses, he turns them yellow. My newspapers, too." She shooed Lobo away and sat down in front of the audience of men. "Haven't you ever seen an old lady get her blood pressure before?" she asked, the veins showing on her neck. I couldn't tell if this was on purpose or not. It raised her blood pressure to 130 over 75 but offered the diagnosis of normal.

She tried again, this time holding her breath. Her cheeks looked like the trumpet player's in the Tejano band. But, before the machine could get a reading, Beatriz seemed to faint. Only the blood pressure cuff stopped her steel-gray head from hitting the floor. A red band formed around her droopy biceps.

Hector, her nephew and my second cousin, who sometimes acted as if he was still fighting in Iraq, stepped forward to prop her upright and offer her a drink of his beer. She took one swallow before she realized what it was and stuck her tongue out. Hector reclaimed the can and held it over Lobo's head. The dog knew the drill. He tilted his head back and began licking at the air. His tongue gained speed when the trickle of beer started.

"You should pray to Saint Simon for temperance," Grumbelina said. She turned back to Paramo. "I need something new for my blood pressure. It is still too high."

I was surprised that she admitted it.

"It's probably all those tomatoes," Beatriz said. She leaned on Hector's shoulder near the window. When Grumbelina didn't respond, Beatriz said, "Asking people to put tomatoes on your grave will make you smell like garbage."

Grumbelina asked Paramo for some white fifty-hour candles.

Pouting now, Beatriz added, "Diamanta, rest her innocent soul, deserves better than your Yaqui altars and unnatural tomatoes."

We all waited. Grumbelina seemed like she was going to ignore Beatriz, but to criticize how a mother continues to grieve her lost infant, her *angelita*, after all these years.

"Crazy woman." Grumbelina turned to address Beatriz. "Your tongue is as useless as your flowers."

"You should accept the way of the Lord," Beatriz interrupted her.

"You did not lose a perfect baby girl. Jewel of my heart. You know nothing. Nothing! You and your greedy Anglo church."

This startled the two kids not from Calle Guadalupe, with chipped black fingernails and spiked doggie collars, who had skulked in and were fingering the sugar skulls. Upon discovering that Paramo didn't take credit cards, they apologetically rifled through their chained wallets and riveted pockets for crumbles of money—singles, a twenty, fives. So much money. Meanwhile, Hector succeeded in leading Beatriz through the door. Outside, most of the men had left to go home for dinner. I knew Paramo wanted to close up and get to his mother's to eat, and so did I. To my boyfriend's mother's house, that is. I could hear Lobo licking at the empty beer cans on the ground.

Grumbelina paid Paramo for the candles, some reddish powder, and dried leaves that looked like oregano. He had no rhubarb. As we were leaving, the storm clouds that had been beyond the mountains for days seemed to thicken in the sunset. Rain would be better than the sprinkles we had been getting, though sprinkles were always just enough to make the carwash busy and the tips good. Cars came in speckled with dirt and left shiny as mirrors—until they hit the first puddle down the road.

Grumbelina and I walked in silence. I wanted to say something. Again, I had no idea what to say, so I just stayed beside her. She didn't seem to notice me until she had a hand on her gate, ready to open it.

"I have some tomatoes for you to take to your mother," Grumbelina said, grabbing me by the elbow.

I had no choice but to follow her into the yard. Lobo rushed past my knees, his fur catching at the fabric of my dress.

Grumbelina picked up a rumpled, brown sack from the patio and gave it to me. "You will take these to your mother." She stared into my eyes and put an invasive hand on my pregnant belly. "Don't disappoint me."

My mother pulls a missing-child postcard and grocery fliers from our mailbox before answering. "Such foolishness." She doesn't look at me.

"No, Elena is right," Beatriz says. "Tomato plants. Those unnatural ones that never turn red." She bends over to prop a thick, glass bottle from the Herbaria between her ankles and then tries to lean on our pig-wire fence. The fence buckles under the pressure, and Beatriz almost loses her balance.

They are clucking about my observance of Día de los Muertos, especially my efforts to erect a garden altar for Grumbelina and the offerings, *ofrendas*, of her *d'Or* tomatoes and other fresh foods I'm assembling.

The children—my baby brother, my little Chencha, and other people's *niños* who I mind all day—tackle each other in the dirt-filled sandbox next to our peeling statue of Our Lady of Guadalupe. I hold the hose and squirt any child who dares run past me toward the garden. Mild November temperatures have finally taken their hold on the desert, but I still have lots of takers. The children are either wet, covered with sandy mud, or screaming.

Two years ago, just before I had Chencha, I took those tomatoes to my mother—minus the one I ate on the street, which wasn't as memorable as the one handed to me earlier that night by Grumbelina. I approached the trailer, but I couldn't step up to the door. I passed by, scanning yards and windows to see if anyone was watching. I found myself pressing the tomato bag against my hip with a rigid hand. I turned the corner and decided to walk around the old block.

When I was little and couldn't cross the street, I would ride my mother's three-speed bike round and round that block. My feet only reached halfway on the pedals, so I had to push and pull with my bare toes. The gears clicked one-two-three, one-two. . . .That blue bike has always been rusty, but it's worse now. It has been sitting behind the trailer for years. I bet my old boyfriend could fix it with a little oil and new tires. I'll have to ask him the next time he brings a Central College toy to our Chencha. She could ride behind me in the child seat.

I remember re-approaching the trailer that night, wondering if I should knock on the screen door or if I could dare to just walk in, or even leave. My hands felt damp. At first, I thought it was because I was nervous, but it turned out to be the tomatoes. I had crushed them until their juice had soaked through the paper bag. I was afraid to look at them, much less present them to my mother.

But there she was, at the kitchen window washing the dinner dishes. I could smell honey-sweet sopapillas. She seemed to look at me without acknowledging my presence, like the glass-eyed Virgin statue in the yard. I felt safe hidden in the shadow of a neighbor's citrus tree, yet I stepped out into the streetlight.

Mother disappeared from the window and reappeared in the doorway.

"Mamá?" was all I could say. I tried not to cry. My mother always wept in frustration over the "daddies," like my father, who stayed for a few years before deserting her. Even my Luis had said he might want to see other girls, college girls.

"Elena's going to destroy the marigolds I planted around her tomatoes," my mother says.

"You should leave them alone," Beatriz says to me. "Keep the bugs away."

"When I take down the altar, I'll mulch the petals around the tomatoes," I say. Now, they are my tomatoes, although the children helped me plant other vegetables, too. I, like Grumbelina, believe the only worthwhile plants to cultivate are things you can eat—peppers, chilies, corn.... chickens. My mother and Beatriz, on the other hand, devote their time to flowers, especially those for their Mormon stake house. Our fence always crawls with blood-red roses, and flowers with Hollywood starlet names strain the beds around the double-wide.

Before Grumbelina's second, and lethal, series of strokes, she had me bring her ripest tomatoes to the county care center so we could extract the seeds. In my mother's yard, a few anemic seedlings survive with only one producing near-perfect golden tomatoes. Chencha tries to help me tend the vines that Lobo keeps peeing on. I watch him sniffing, taking position, and lifting his leg across the yard.

"Look at the wolf," Beatriz says.

Chencha, wearing only a wet daisy-print T-shirt in the afternoon sun, toddles over to Lobo. I resist the urge to spray them both with the hose. She uses the dog's back to help her balance as she lifts her leg. When Lobo moves away, she lands on her palms, but somehow keeps her leg up. Urine drips off her knee and runs down her belly. Before any of us can say a thing, she twists and falls on her heavy bottom, probably on top of one of the struggling tomato plants. Chencha cries and points at the dog.

My mother pulls Chencha to her feet, turning her around to display the pieces of mulch and straw stuck to her cherubic buttocks. She uses junk mail to swat the debris off my girl's bottom, making her cries louder.

"Come here, *bebé*," I say. I feel the grit on her sweaty fingers as she clutches at my arm. I gently sprinkle water on her legs to rinse off the muck, saving her most tender skin for last.

"We've got to take care of those tomatoes," I say. "I promised the best ones to Grumbelina. We want to honor her memory, not baptize her in her grave like your *nana*." I explain to Chencha that the only thing Grumbelina liked more than those tomatoes was a good fight. I pause to consider what fight Grumbelina saw in me.

I look past my mother—who is giving me the glare she usually reserves for aphids—at the red-tile roofs of the South Mountain developments. I envision a skull-faced Grumbelina, still in her cotton housecoat, riding my mother's bike across the freeway overpass. On the handlebars, the plastic basket holds a tiny pink-swaddled newborn whose face I cannot see. The child seat behind Grumbelina overflows with grocery bags of tomatoes so ripe their thick yellow skins are leaking seeds everywhere. She's pedaling fast, and the only reason she slows is to reach behind her hip for a tomato. She throws, but the flesh can't cross over. I detect a slight riffling of dirt in the garden near Lobo, who bolts under the trailer. Only then do I notice the tourists snapping pictures of me and Grumbelina's altar.

"Ten dollars," Beatriz says, her hand outstretched.

FUTURE DUST

BY JARED WALLS

There's probably a German word for the entire situation,
but as I walk into the Bridal Palace,
the glass doors shining teeth,
I can't help but stare at the dresses—hanged ghosts,
floating just above the femur-high elevation of fog.

The sequins, crooked spines of stars,
stitched to silk from a generation of worms—
I envision the future dust of a thousand attics,
revealing spindles of noonlight—
dresses packed into trunks like Niagara stuntmen
along with souvenirs from Albuquerque.

The girl behind the counter twists her ponytail,
a geyser from the top of her skull—
she looks at me as if I just fed her a knife.

I step back outside and stare across the highway:
six lanes as wide as the water that kept this continent a secret.
A woman in the parking lot, woodfire hair,
pulls smoke from her cigarette, flicks it onto the blonde grass.
I look back through the door—like a vending machine thief,
the girl reaches up one of the dresses.

PSALM: GOLDENEYE

BY B.J. BEST

In a vast field of white, you are the orange sky.
In a room of computers, you are a scientist with his silver
    flask of wine.
A knife in a sewer, the underground traffic of mice, the
    deteriorating orbit and yaw—
You have my dossier. I surrender my weapons—
I want your laser to burn through my bones.

CONTRIBUTORS

MARTIN ARNOLD teaches in the English Department at Guilford College. He is currently the Associate Poetry Editor at storySouth. He earned an MFA from The University of North Carolina at Greensboro, where he was the poetry editor of *The Greensboro Review*, and an MA from New Mexico State University. His poems have been published in *Crazyhorse*, *Poetry East*, *Denver Quarterly*, *Mississippi Review*, and elsewhere.

B.J. BEST holds an MFA from Washington University in St. Louis. His work has appeared recently in *Cream City Review*, *North American Review*, and *Quarterly West*. His chapbooks *Mead Lake*, *This*, and *Crap* are available from Centennial Press, and a third, *Drag: Twenty Short Poems about Smoking*, is forthcoming.

PAUL BOGARD savors the night sky from the shores of Lake Superior in Ashland, Wisconsin, where he teaches at Northland College.

JACLYN DWYER'S fiction has appeared or is forthcoming in *3:AM Magazine*, *The Cortland Review*, *The Bend*, and *thirty under thirty anthology*. Her interview with A.M. Homes is published in *Notre Dame Review*. She received Honorable Mention in Writecorner Press Short Fiction Contest 2008 and was nominated for AWP Intro to Journals Contest 2009. Jaclyn was accepted into Florida State University's Creative Writing Program where she plans to pursue her Ph.D.

GARY FINCKE'S nonfiction account of his son's life in the rock band Breaking Benjamin, *Amp'd*, was published by Michigan State University Press, which will also publish his memoir, *The Canals of Mars*, in 2010.

GREG FRASER is the author of two books of poetry, *Strange Pietà* (Texas Tech, 2003) and *Answering the Ruins* (Northwestern, 2009), and co-author, with Chad Davidson, of *Poetry Writing: Creative-Critical Approaches* (Palgrave-Macmillan, 2008). The recipient of a grant from the NEA,

Fraser serves as associate professor of English at the University of West Georgia, outside Atlanta.

JENNY HANNING is from Maine, but lives in Austin, Texas, where she is a MA canidate in fiction at the University of Texas at Austin. Her fiction and poetry have appeared in *Cimarron Review, Shenandoah, Third Coast,* and others.

KEITH MONTESANO currently teaches English at Virginia Commonwealth University. Other poems have appeared or are forthcoming in *Hayden's Ferry Review, River Styx, American Literary Review, Sonora Review, Passages North, Third Coast, Madison Review, Nimrod,* and elsewhere. His first manuscript has been a finalist in recent contests, but is still looking for a publisher.

RACHEL NEWCOMB is an assistant professor of anthropology at Rollins College in Winter Park, Florida. She holds an MA in the Writing Seminars from Johns Hopkins University, and her work has recently appeared or is forthcoming in *Clackamas Literary Review, Kennesaw Review, Painted Bride Quarterly,* and *Anthropology and Humanism.* Her ethnography, *Women of Fes:Ambiguities of Urban Life in Morocco,* will be published by University of Pennsylvania Press in December 2008.

JOHN NICHOLS was born in 1940, in Berkeley, California. He attended Hamilton College, in upstate New York, where he played collegiate ice hockey, ran cross country, and started in earnest as a novelist. An accomplished screenwriter, photographer, and cartoonist, as well as an avid hiker, Nichols lives in Taos, New Mexico, his home for the past forty years.

JOHN NIZALOWSKI is the author of a multi-genre work entitled *Hooking the Sun* on Farolito Press. His writings have also appeared in *Puerto del Sol, Weber: the Contemporary West, Bloomsbury Review, Blueline, Convergence, Albany Review, Creosote, The Listening Eye,* and elsewhere. Currently, he resides in Grand Junction, Colorado, where he teaches creative writing and mythology at Mesa State College.

MELISSA OLSON-PETRIE has served as fiction editor for *Hayden's Ferry Review* at Arizona State University. Her work has been published in *Porcupine Literary Arts Magazine.* Other publication credits include reporting for a daily newspaper in Scottsdale, Arizona, and her continued writing for university research magazines. She lives in Cedarburg, Wisconsin, with her husband and two sons.

STEVEN RAMIREZ is from El Paso, Texas. He has two wonderful parents—Art and Irma—and two brothers who he'll go ahead and call wonderful as well. There have been several special dogs in his life. Steven is a graduate of the Iowa Writers Workshop and resides in the Midwest.

YELIZAVETA P. RENFRO'S short story collection, *A Catalogue of Everything in the World*, won the 2008 St. Lawrence Book Award and is forthcoming from Black Lawrence Press in 2010. Her fiction and nonfiction have appeared in *Glimmer Train Stories*, *North American Review*, *Alaska Quarterly Review*, *Witness*, *So to Speak*, and the anthology *A Stranger Among Us: Stories of Cross Cultural Collision and Connection* (University of Illinois Press/OV Books, 2008). She earned an M.F.A. in Creative Writing from George Mason University and is completing her Ph.D. in English at the University of Nebraska-Lincoln.

SUZANNE SBARGE was born in Hartford, Connecticut in 1965. She has lived in Albuquerque, New Mexico since 1989. Her work has been exhibited in over 50 group exhibitions and 12 solo shows since the late 1980s. It is in the collections of over 75 local, national and international collectors, and is represented at galleries across the United States. She received her B.A. degree in Art History and Studio Arts from Barnard College in New York City and her M.A. degree in Art Education from the University of New Mexico. She has also studied studio arts at L'Ecole des Beaux Arts in Toulouse, France; Syracuse University in Florence, Italy; The Art Students' League in New York City; University of Connecticut; University of Massachusetts; as well as Anderson Ranch in Colorado, Penland School of Crafts in North Carolina and Vermont Studio Center. In addition to her own work, she is a gallery director, curator, graphic designer, writer and arts consultant. She is currently Executive Director of 516 ARTS in Albuquerque.

MAUREEN SEATON is the author of thirteen books, both solo and collaborative. Her recent publications are *Sextalks, to Girls*, a memoir from the University of Wisconsin Press, 2008; *Cave of the Yellow Volkswagen*, poems from Carnegie Mellon University Press, 2009; and a chapbook, *America Loves Carney*, from Sow's Ear, 2009.

TATJANA SOLI was born in Salzburg, Austria. She attended Stanford University and the Warren Wilson MFA Program. Her stories have appeared in *StoryQuarterly, Confrontation, Gulf Coast, Other Voices, Nimrod, Third Coast, Carolina Quarterly, Sonora Review,* and *North Dakota Quarterly,* among other publications. Her work has been twice listed in the 100 Distinguished Stories in *Best American Short Stories* and nominated for the Pushcart Prize. She was awarded the Pirate's Alley Faulkner Prize, the Dana Award, and scholarships to the Sewanee Writers' Conference and Bread Loaf Writers' Conference. Currently she teaches through the Gotham Writers' Workshop. In 2009, her work will be a featured reading at L.A.'s New Short Fiction Series.

MARY HELEN SPECHT was born and raised in Abilene, Texas. Her work has been published in numerous magazines including *Southwest Review, Florida Review, Colorado Review,* and *Night Train,* where she won the Richard Yates Short Story Award. The recipient of a Fulbright grant to Nigeria and the Dobie Paisano fellowship, Specht currently lives and writes in Austin, Texas.

JARED WALLS is in the MFA program at Texas State University, where he serves as poetry editor of *Front Porch Journal.* He lives in Austin with his wife Caroline.

$1000 FIRST PRIZE!

Blue Mesa Review Fiction Contest

Get Published!
The winning entry will be published in the 2010 issue of *Blue Mesa Review*.

Please include: A SASE and a $15 check made payable to UNM-BMR for each story submitted.

Submissions must be postmarked by

December 31, 2009
and must not exceed 7,000 words.

All contest participants will recieve a copy of the contest issue.

SEND ENTRIES TO:

Blue Mesa Review
Creative Writing Program
University of New Mexico
MSC03-2170 Humanities 274
Albuquerque, NM 87131-0001

Guest judges to be announced
For more information please contact bmrinfo@unm.edu